Vignettes of Virtue

Short Stories of the American Restoration Movement

Frank Richey

© Frank Richey, 2010
ALL RIGHTS RESERVED. No part of this book may be reproduced in any form or by any means, without written permission from the author.

Cover
Old Mulkey Meetinghouse, Tompkinsville, Kentucky.
Used by permission of the State of Kentucky,
Department of Parks
Photograph by Frank Richey, 2004

ISBN 978-0-9816519-2-7

Published by
Cypress Creek Book Company
Florence, Alabama

Dedication

This book is dedicated to Wayne Kilpatrick, my mentor in the study of restoration history, who taught me, answered my questions, helped me build a library, and is my friend.

Acknowledgements

This book has been the result of my love for history and love of the Lord's church. I have had an interest in history since I was a boy. My first job in the field of education was as a history teacher. After four years in the classroom, I spent twenty-seven years as a principal and preached on a part-time basis. This left little or no time for the study of restoration history.

When I retired from the field of education, I took a course in restoration history taught by Wayne Kilpatrick, professor of history at Heritage Christian University. I fell in love with the study of restoration history and was fortunate enough to live in the same town as Wayne, who has guided me in this study and has been an encouragement to me. Together we have made numerous trips to restoration history sites, cemeteries, and the Disciples of Christ Historical Society in Nashville, Tennessee. Wayne has helped me accumulate books on restoration history and has always been available to me for help and assistance.

A special thanks to Larry Whitehead, editor of the *Alabama Restoration Journal*, who chose me as a co-editor. He has encouraged me to write, has been a constant inspiration to me, and is one with whom I speak almost daily about restoration history projects. Without his encouragement, this material would not have been written.

Also, I appreciate Earl Kimbrough, a man with whom I am honored to be associated, and who has been an inspiration to me. He is an excellent historian, and has written for several journals for half a century.

I appreciate those who volunteered to edit this book, and their many hours of work on this project is much appreciated. Lavaga Logan, Mary Hamrick, and my wife, Julia, read the manuscript and made suggestions.

Bennie Johns has been great to help me with layout questions and in assisting me with the setup of the book. He is always willing to help, and I call on him often.

I have always been a person that had rather talk than write. I have been encouraged in my writing as a result of the responsibility to write and edit a monthly bulletin, which is a part of the work of the church for which I preach. Many people have told me over the years that they appreciate my work with the bulletin and have encouraged me. My wife, Julia, has encouraged me also. She is my greatest critic and counselor. Without her proofreading and suggestions, my writings would never see the light of day.

Contents

Page

Introduction	9
The Indian and the Bible	15
Baptism of an Old Man	18
A Contested Baptism	25
Gospel Meeting on Cypress Creek	29
Benjamin Lynn: A Man of Naïve Faith	33
John Mulkey: Standing on the Bible Alone	37
The Carriage that Converted a Town	52
Baptism without Consent	55
Raccoon John Smith and the Campbellites	60
The Old Upping Stone	62
Emotionalism in Worship in the 19th Century	66
Dr. Lewis Clark Chisholm.	71
The Rise and Demise of Jesse B. Ferguson	81
The Gospel Preacher Condemned to Death by Hanging	98
Saved by Uncle Sandy	104
General Richard Montgomery Gano, CSA	108
From Preacher to President	120
In Search of J. H. Hundley	137
Memory of a Forgotten Infant	146
The Wedding that Never Happened	153
Alexander Campbell's Family Connection to Alabama	157
John Henry: The Walking Bible	169
T. B. Larimore-The Preacher	182
"Parson" George Ricks	198
The Murder of James Madison Pickens	209
Final Word	231

Introduction

The Great Awakening on the American Frontier

The American restoration movement had its beginning on the western frontier about the start of the nineteenth century. Prior to this time, religion in America was dominated by the older mainline religions of the Episcopalians, Presbyterians, Methodists, and to a lesser extent, the Catholics.

There seemed to be a religious lull in America after the Revolutionary War. The time was ripe for an explosion of religious fervor. This intense interest in religion had its beginning in a most unlikely place—a den of thieves, robbers, murderers, and counterfeiters in Logan County, Kentucky.

A Methodist preacher, Peter Cartwright, wrote:

> When my father moved to (Logan County), it was called 'Rogues Harbor.' Here many refugees, from almost all parts of the Union, fled to escape justice or punishment; for although there was law, yet it could not be executed, and it was a desperate state of society. Murderers, horse thieves, highway robbers, and counterfeiters fled here till they combined and actually formed a majority. The honest and civil part of the citizens would prosecute these wretched banditti, but they would swear each other clear; and they really put all law at defiance, and carried on such desperate violence and outrage that the honest part of the citizens seemed to be driven to the necessity of uniting and combining together, and taking the law into their own hands, under the name of Regulators. The Regulators hunted, killed, and lynched many of the rogues, until several of them fled, and left for parts unknown.

In 1796, a Presbyterian minister arrived at Red River near Maulding Fort, three miles northeast of Adairville, Kentucky. His name was James McGready. He took charge of three churches: the Red River, Muddy River, and Gasper River Churches, and for the next three years preached without much success. But in 1799, a great revival broke out when dozens of members in the Red River and Gasper River congregations were "slain in the spirit." This was attributed to a direct operation of the Holy Spirit, and curiosity and interest in religion soared. In June 1800, several hundred met for a communion service at the Red River meeting house. People came from a hundred mile radius to attend the four day meeting. People were praying, rejoicing, and shedding tears of joy. McGready said he "went through the house shouting and exhorting with all possible ecstasy and energy, and the floor was soon covered by the slain."

Not only was James McGready present to preach, but Presbyterian preachers, Mr. Rankin, Mr. Hodge, and William McGee, along with Methodist preacher, John McGee, brother of William, were present. On Monday morning of the meeting, while Mr. Hodge was preaching, a woman began to shout and cry loudly. After this, the crowd would not leave and John McGee felt that the Holy Spirit wanted him to preach. However, the woman continued to shout, and McGee was too agitated to preach. He then decided that the Lord God was speaking to their hearts.

News of this meeting and its unusual happenings spread like wildfire through every settlement in the region, and as the religious fervor heightened, people from throughout the area were crying out for mercy and turning to God. As the meeting progressed, the excitement grew more intense and the crowds rushed about singing, shouting, laughing, and calling upon those present to repent. There was a multitude that had come together. Many were thought to have been "spiritually slain," some were unable to move or speak, and some lay quietly on the ground. There was chanting of hymns, sobs, shrieks, shouts, and sudden spasms that unexpectedly dashed people to the ground. The people had reached the highest peak of religious excitement. Of course, the Holy Spirit was given credit for the emotional outburst and unusual happenings.

The preachers and those attending were impressed that the religious fervor continued to be heightened. Many of those of the Presbyterian belief cast off the doctrines of Calvinism, especially the doctrine of total depravity and that they must be of the "elect" in order to be saved. They believed that anyone could be saved that turned to God. This meeting was the beginning of the "Great Awakening" on the American frontier.

In the fall of 1800, a young Presbyterian preacher rode a hundred miles to hear from McGready about the "Red River Revival." This young man was Barton Warren Stone. Near the end of the next summer in August 1801, Stone arranged a similar meeting at the Cane Ridge meetinghouse near Lexington, Kentucky. This meeting was so successful that Stone estimated as many as twenty to thirty thousand attended the meeting. This was approximately a third of the population of Kentucky at that time. This meeting was even more successful than the Red River meeting, with similar results. In Barton Stone's autobiography, Stone described the emotionalism that took place at Cane Ridge and listed some of the "exercises," as he called them. Among these were falling down, the jerks, dancing, barking, laughing, running, and singing.

Barton Stone

While the logical mind has trouble explaining these "exercises," the emotional mind will quickly attribute such things to a direct operation of the Holy Spirit, ushering in a "Great Awakening" of religion in a spiritually starved western frontier. However, Stone concludes this story by saying, "there were many eccentricities, and much fanaticism in this excitement." Fanaticism is defined as "irrational zeal." Irrational is the antithesis of the ability to reason, or of being of a sound mind.

These two meetings, the Red River Meeting and the Cane Ridge Meeting, served to cause an intense religious fervor in the West. They also served to cause many to question their former religious beliefs and to seek salvation based on the Bible rather than on the mainline religious teachings of the day.

One who questioned where he was religiously was the young Presbyterian preacher, Barton W. Stone. By 1803, Stone became convinced that in order to faithfully serve God, man must return to the teachings of the New Testament and shun the religious doctrines, manuals, and disciplines of the day. When Stone withdrew from the Springfield Presbytery, he determined that it should die—that men should not join themselves into such a religious organization. In 1804, along with five other ministers, Stone signed the "Last Will and Testament of the Springfield Presbytery." They wrote:

> We will, that the church of Christ assume her native right of internal government—try her candidates for the ministry, as to their soundness in the faith, acquaintance with experimental religion, gravity and aptness to teach; and admit no other proof of their authority, but Christ speaking in them. We will that the church of Christ look up to the Lord of the harvest to send forth labourers into his harvest; and that she resume her primitive right of trying those who say they are Apostles, and are not.

When the Springfield Presbytery met its death, those who killed it were determined to restore New Testament Christianity. This meant turning to the Bible alone for authority and no longer following the creeds of men and orthodoxy of the mainline religions of the day. When Barton Stone asked, "What shall we call ourselves?" Rice Haggard spoke up and said, "We should call ourselves Christians." Interestingly, Rice Haggard suggested the same name to James O'Kelly ten years earlier when O'Kelly broke with the Methodist church.

But what was to be the name of the church of the Bible—the church built by Jesus Christ? Stone felt that the name, "Church of Christ" should be used because the name was both scriptural (Romans 16:16) and showed ownership by Christ.

Many antagonists refer to the members of churches of Christ as "Campbellites." This erroneous and derogatory name is used out of ignorance or prejudice. Alexander Campbell was a boy in Ireland when the American restoration movement began. Campbell was a boy when the Rock Springs Church of Christ began in 1805 in Celina, Tennessee. He was a boy when Benjamin Lynn left the Baptist church and promoted New Testament Christianity in 1808. He was a young man on his way to America when John Mulkey left the Mill Creek Baptist Association to seek the old paths. Campbell had not reached America when the Rocky Springs church was established in Jackson County, Alabama. Examples of this point are numerous. It is estimated that there were over one hundred restoration churches with a membership of thirteen thousand by the year 1810—the year Alexander Campbell preached his first sermon.

Why then the name, "Campbellites"? Alexander Campbell was a very talented, brilliant, and educated man who promoted the return to New Testament Christianity. For most of his life, he published journals read by and accepted by many seeking religious truth. These papers were *The Christian Baptist* (1823-1829) and the *Millennial Harbinger* (1830 to his death in 1866, and then was continued two more years). The influence of these papers, Campbell's many printed debates, his numerous preaching excursions throughout the country, and his eloquence as a speaker gained him a reputation as a champion for the restoration movement. Campbell spoke of those who would use the name, "Campbellites."

> We do protest against christening the gospel of Jesus and the Christian religion, by the name of any mortal man. To carry the principle out, we ought to call every man's sentiments by his name. Because we have disclaimed creeds, names, and sects, our adversaries seem to take a pleasure in designating our writings and speeches by the name creed, Campbellism, theory, system, etc. This is both unmanly and unchristian. Men, fond of nicknaming, are generally weak in reason, argument, and proof (*Millennial Harbinger*, 1830, page 118).

In January 1832, the movement to return to New Testament Christianity that began with Barton Stone and the movement that began with Alexander Campbell came together in a unity meeting at the old Hill Street Church in Lexington, Kentucky. Many denominationalists, fearing the growth of this group seeking a return to the Bible, were now threatened by their numbers.

The early 1800s marked the beginning of the American restoration movement—a movement to restore the New Testament church based on the Bible alone. Without the use of manmade doctrines, these people took a giant step backwards—all the way to the Bible and to the Bible alone for authority.

But sadly, today many churches that claim their roots in the restoration movement have abandoned those restoration roots, and are now hardly recognizable as being a part of the restoration movement. As we consider the lives of those who have struggled and died for the cause of Christ, let us be moved to imitate their commitment to the truth.

Chapter 1

The Indian and the Bible

In the early 1800s, there were many attempts by various denominations to reach the Indians of many tribes. Before the government seized Indian lands and Indians were forced onto western reservations, there were many tribes located in almost every state. In the South, the Cherokee Indians were the predominant tribe in North Carolina, northern Georgia, and northern Alabama. However, almost all Cherokees were relocated to Oklahoma. This relocation resulted in the *Trail of Tears*, the forced relocation of the Indian tribes to the west of the Mississippi River.

In his 1829 inaugural address, President Andrew Jackson set a policy to relocate eastern Indians. In 1830, it was endorsed when Congress passed the Indian Removal Act to force those remaining to move west of the Mississippi. Between 1830 and 1850, about 100,000 American Indians living between Michigan, Louisiana, and Florida moved west after the U.S. government coerced treaties or used the U.S. Army against those resisting. Most Cherokees, including Chief John Ross, did not believe that they would be forced to move. In May 1838, Federal troops and state militias began the roundup of the Cherokees into stockades. In spite of warnings to troops to treat the Cherokees kindly, the roundup proved harrowing. Families were separated—the elderly and ill forced out at gunpoint—and people were given only moments to collect cherished possessions. White looters followed, ransacking homesteads as Cherokees were led away.

By March 1839, all survivors had arrived in the West. No one knows how many died throughout the ordeal, but the trip was especially hard on infants, children, and the elderly. Missionary Dr. Elizur Butler, who accompanied the

Cherokees, estimated that over 4,000 died—nearly a fifth of the Cherokee population.

Many of the Cherokees were peaceful. They did, however, join with Andrew Jackson to fight the Creeks and helped defeat them at the Battle of Horseshoe Bend in South Alabama. The reward for their assistance was to be relocated, driven from their homes, and for many, to their deaths. This is why a young Tennessean named David Crockett became a political opponent of the most famous politician of the day, Andrew Jackson. Crockett had been a scout for Jackson's army when they fought in the Indian wars of 1814, and seeing how Jackson "rewarded" the Cherokees made him sick.

It was in this early period of westward expansion that a clan of Cherokees lived in Northeast Alabama in what is now Jackson County, Alabama. The Methodists were concerned about the souls of the Indians in this area and sent missionaries to the Indians to convert them. Many Cherokees, like Sequoyah, the Cherokee who developed the Cherokee alphabet, had learned not only to speak English but to read it as well. On this particular occasion, a Methodist missionary gave a Bible to an old Indian who could read English. The missionary told the old Indian that he would return the next year and discuss the Bible with him. For the next year, the old Indian read the Bible through and through with a desire to do what God wanted him to do. True to his word, the Methodist missionary returned to the Indian camp a year later and found the man to whom he had given the Bible. The following conversation is reported to have taken place.

>"Did you read the Bible I gave you," inquired the missionary.
>
>"Yes," answered the Indian, "and I want to be baptized."
>
>Thinking this was wonderful, the Methodist missionary invited the Indian to his tent and filled a bowl with water.

"What are you going to do with that?" asked the Indian.

"Why, I'm going to baptize you," replied the missionary.

"You are going to baptize me in that?"

"Yes," responded the missionary.

"Then you gave me the wrong Bible," said the Indian.

The old Indian, without any prejudicial teaching from various denominations, realized that in order to be baptized as the people in the Bible were baptized, he had to be immersed. He could not be baptized in a bowl of water.

Without the benefit of studying church history, without the benefit of knowing that sprinkling was introduced to the practice of baptism several hundred years after the New Testament church, this man simply read his Bible and realized that baptism was by immersion.

The other fact the old Indian learned by studying the Bible on his own was that baptism is necessary in order to comply with the will of God for man's salvation. The old Indian had no problem understanding that he should "repent and be baptized for remission of sins" (Acts 2:38).

Chapter 2

Baptism of an Old Man

When Benjamin Franklin Hall read the Campbell-McCalla debate in the spring of 1826, his life was changed forever. By chance, B. F. Hall came across this recently printed book in the cabin of some friends on Line Creek near Gamaliel, Kentucky. Hall could not restrain himself from preaching what he had learned from this book—the ancient doctrine of baptism for remission of sins—so suppressed by the denominations and theologians of the day, the simple New Testament doctrine had, for the most part, been forgotten. The statement made by Campbell during the debate simply read:

> I have affirmed that baptism 'saves us,' that it 'washes away sins.' Well, Peter and Paul have said so before me. If it was not criminal in them to say so, it cannot be criminal in me. When Ananias said unto Paul, 'Arise, and be baptized, and wash away thy sins, calling on the name of the Lord,' I suppose Paul believed him, and arose, was baptized, and washed away his sins. When he was baptized, he must have believed that his sins were now washed away in some sense that they were not before (Campbell, A Public Discussion on Christian Baptism, p. 116).

Campbell, quoting Acts 2:38, captivated the mind of Hall. Never before had he thought of how one became a Christian in light of this passage. Hall was determined to share this message. He wrote:

> I began to read it with fixed attention. The interest deepened as I proceeded. The light began to dawn, nay, it flashed upon my mind; and ere I had

concluded the argument, I was a full convert to the teaching of baptism for remission of sins. I sprang to my feet in an ecstasy and cried out, 'Eureka! Eureka!' I have found it; I have found it. And I had found it. I had found the key-stone in the gospel arch, which had been set aside and ignored by the builders. I had found the long-lost link in the chain of gospel obedience.

The first person he taught baptism for remission of sins was a woman he met on the way home to his father's house. Hall wrote:

> The night before I reached my father's, I stayed with a brother whose wife was not a disciple. I found, however, that she was greatly concerned about her soul. I presented to her the gospel, and exhorted her, as she seemed to be a true penitent, to be baptized for the remission of her sins. She received the word with readiness of mind and, like the Pentecostians, rejoiced that she had learned the way of salvation. I baptized her a few days afterwards. She dedicated the remainder of her life to the service of the Lord, and died some years since in the triumphs of faith (Hall, B. F., Unpublished biography).

Hall went on to say that in July he presented the same sentiments to a number of people in the Georgetown, Kentucky area, but the brethren insisted that he should not preach this at their meetings. Hall did, however, teach in private what he had learned about the importance of baptism for remission of sins.

His interest in the doctrine of baptism for remission of sins seemed so plain to Hall. At this time, he conversed with Barton Stone on the subject. He wrote in his autobiography:

> [T]hat he had introduced it early in the present century, that it was like throwing ice water on the people; that it froze all their warmth out, and came

well nigh driving vital religion out of the country, and would have done it, if he had not resisted from preaching it. He said he had preached it at different places and to different congregations, and that the same results followed. Finally, he abandoned it altogether. I asked him why he had preached it at all? He answered, because he found it in the Scriptures.

Hall went on to say:

> I gave him, however, to distinctly understand that I fully believed it to be the truth, and that I was resolved to preach it; and that, if any of the brethren rejected it, I would tell them 'brother Stone says it is taught in the Scriptures.' This made him laugh. He then pleasantly remarked I was so hardheaded that he could not do anything with me, and he saw I was determined to have my own way. He afterwards requested me in a serious tone not to broach that idea in Georgetown. But I did not promise, for my soul was full of it.

In the fall of 1826, Hall started for Alabama. On his way, he attended a camp meeting at Mill Creek near Tompkinsville, Kentucky. During this meeting, Hall preached baptism for remission of sins. He said that when he concluded the meeting, "I then invited all who wished to be baptized for the remission of their sins to come forward. Five, I think, seated themselves as suggested. I took their confessions in the hearing of a large congregation." Hall stated that it was "between 11 and 12 o'clock, and four of those who had made the confession, wished to be baptized the same hour."

Hall says that after this meeting he went directly to Jackson County, Alabama, where he preached in a camp meeting on Crow's Creek, among the hills bordering on the line between Tennessee and Alabama. Hall wrote:

> I delivered a discourse on Romans 10:1-10, in which I presented the elements of the gospel—its facts, commands and promises, and urged immediate compliance with its provisions in order to (have) remission of sins. I invited persons forward to confess with their lips what in their hearts they believed.

Hall said several came forward, but he made particular mention of an old man with tears streaming down his face, coming forward to accept baptism for remission of sins. He wrote:

> Among them was a venerable gentleman with a good face and fine broad, high-retreating forehead. He arose almost instantly the invitation was given. He supported with a cane his tottering frame, bent under the weight of many years, and stepped forward, and reached me his bony hand, the tears coursing down his furrowed cheeks.

Hall's other account said:

> Steadying himself with his staff, and reached me his thin and palsied hand, tears at the same time gushing from his eyes, and his whole frame shaking with deep emotion.
>
> At the conclusion of the song, the old man asked if he could say a few words. When given permission to speak, he said, 'Friends, I have asked permission to say a few words. You see I am an old man. I am upwards of seventy years of age. From my youth, I have been anxious to be a Christian. I have always attended religious meetings, and listened attentively to the preaching, anxious to learn what I must do to be saved. When I heard of this meeting, my first impulse was to attend it. But then I thought of my age and infirmity, and the distance, about seventy miles, and I remembered that I had never heard anything that I could understand that I must do to be saved, and it was not likely I would be more fortunate, should I come to this meeting, and I

almost abandoned the idea of making the attempt. Then again, I remembered my great age and declining life, and knew I could not live much longer, and the thought of dying without religion was horrible. These reflections armed me with resolution to undertake the long and fatiguing journey, with the faint hope that maybe, I shall hear something that will give me hope and comfort in death. I devoutly thank God that I am here, and that I have been permitted to hear the sermon today. It is the first time in life that I have heard, so that I could understand, what I must do to become a Christian. Young friends, if I had, when I was of your age, heard the discourse to which you have just listened, I would have then become a Christian.'

The old man added, "If I had, when young, heard the sermon just delivered I doubt not I should now have been a veteran of the Cross, instead of being, as I am, an aged sinner."

At this point, the old man broke down weeping and Hall wrote:

> [I]t was enough to move a heart of stone. The confessions of the weeping penitents was (sic) taken and the group made their way to the water only a few paces away, to be immersed into Christ Jesus.
> As the old gentleman emerged from the liquid grave a smile played over his features, blending with his tears; he clapped together his thin hands. As the aged gentleman came out of the water, a holy joy lit up his countenance, and a manly smile played upon his features; he clasped his bony hands together and said. 'Praised be the Lord that I ever saw this day! I can return home and die in peace, for I have found what I have been seeking for all my life.'

Hall added that the old man said:

Thanks be to God for the assurance I now feel that my sins are forgiven! I have believed his word, and, as I trust, have from the heart complied with his prescribed conditions of pardon, and, confiding in his word of promise, I rejoice to be assured of my acceptance with my adorable Savior. I can now return home contented and happy, and occupy the few remaining days I may yet live on earth in making ready for the life to come. Friends, one and all, farewell. Our next meeting will be at the judgment. May I hope to see you all in heaven? At this affecting talk of the old man, many wept. It was the last day of the meeting. The congregation soon dispersed. I assisted the old man on his horse, and bade him a final adieu, and never heard of him afterwards, but hope to meet him in heaven. O what meetings and greetings, and joyful recognitions there will be in the spirit world!

The story of the baptism of this old man raises a number of questions. First, who was this old man? We do not know. Secondly, where was he from? Again, we do not know the answer. Thirdly, why did the old man, obviously in ill health, make a seventy mile trip to hear Hall preach? We simply do not know. But to this question we might speculate an answer. Could God's hand have been in this? Could it have been that this old sinner, who for many years sought to know God's plan for the salvation of man, who had heard many sermons from many ministers, realized that there was more to salvation than just praying to God? Did God provide a door of opportunity for him to obey the gospel of Christ before his demise? Even a casual observer can see God's hand all over this event. Our Lord said, "Ask, and it will be given to you; seek, and you will find; knock, and it will be opened to you. For everyone who asks receives, and he who seeks finds, and to him who knocks it will be opened" (Matthew 7:7-8). Did the old man do the same thing Saul of Tarsus did in order to be saved? Saul, later called Paul, said of his conversion that Ananias came to him with this message, "Arise and be baptized, and wash away your sins, calling on the name of the Lord" (Acts 22:16). When the old man came up from the watery grave, he had obeyed what Jesus, Peter, and Paul preached.

From Jackson County, Hall made his way to Madison County, Alabama, where he continued to baptize many for the remission of sins. From there, he came to Lauderdale County, Alabama, where he held his well-documented meeting on Cypress Creek. One of those present was James E. Matthews who upon hearing Hall's sermon on the necessity of baptism for remission of sins wrote his old friend, Barton W. Stone, a series of three articles titled *"The Gospel Plan of Saving Sinners,"* published in the *Christian Messenger* in 1828. These articles went a long way in convincing Stone to go back to preaching the necessity of baptism—a message he had taught many years earlier. The articles also convinced many preachers to take a stand for this biblical doctrine and helped to bring about the unity meeting between the Stone and Campbell groups in 1832.

Chapter 3

A Contested Baptism

Dr. B. F. Hall

As mentioned previously, B. F. Hall came to the conclusion that baptism was for the remission of sins, and in the spring of 1826 he began to preach this doctrine as Peter did on the Day of Pentecost. During the summer months, he preached this doctrine in Kentucky, and then made his way to the Rocky Springs community in Jackson County, Alabama, where a meetinghouse had been built about fifteen years earlier. The Rocky Springs church is considered the oldest church of Christ in Alabama. (The church had its beginning about 1811, when William J. Price came to the Antioch community in Jackson County. He began preaching the importance of returning to the New Testament alone for scriptural authority.) Concerning this meeting at Rocky Springs, Hall wrote in his unpublished autobiography:

> Here again I preached the ancient gospel, and immersed for remission of sins some twenty-three persons, among them a James C. Anderson and a brother Russell. They had both been Methodists. Brother Anderson soon became a preacher; and for many years labored through both Ala. and Tenn. He was an efficient preacher, and won many souls to God. He was blind in one eye. He now rests from his labors.

After this meeting at Rocky Springs, Hall held a meeting at Crow's Creek, in Jackson County, Alabama. It was here that he baptized the old man mentioned in the previous chapter.

Hall then made his way west to Madison County, Alabama, and held a meeting in the community of McNutty (sic, McNulty). It was here that a threat was issued by a man whose daughter had responded to Hall's preaching and had decided to be baptized. Hall, in his autobiography, tells of the incident.

> An incident occurred in Alabama, which I will here relate. I, at a meeting above Miridianville (sic), delivered a discourse on the design of baptism and invited persons to confess the Lord. One young lady came forward, and desired to be immersed forthwith. Her mother was dead. Her father, had been a Baptist preacher, but had become an apostate and a wicked man. As we were yet talking about the best place to immerse in a stream nearby, the old man came up to me, and shaking a large hickory cane in my face, told me I must not baptize his daughter. I inquired: 'Why not?' He answered huffishly: 'That is none of your business; but'—shaking his cane again at me, his eyes looking daggers—'you had better not attempt to baptize her'—and his large frame shook with rage. Turning to the young lady, who sat weeping, I asked her if she still desired to be baptized. She said she did. 'Then I will baptize you at all hazards.' I said, and, turning to the audience, designated the place where we would administer the rite. The old man, turning to his daughter, said: 'If you are baptized, you shall never enter my house again while you live.' The poor girl, looking up at me through her tears, said: 'I want to be baptized.' An old brother Griffin, a man well to do in the world, who stood near by, walked up to the agonized girl, and said, 'my daughter, you shall have a home at my house.' We repaired to the water, and I baptized her, the old man offering no resistance. The young lady got into mister Griffin's carriage, and went

home with him. A few days afterwards, her father sent for her to return home. She sent him word she would not go then; but if he would bring a horse and saddle the next Friday, and take her down to a meeting to be held at McNuttytown, she would go home with him after the close of the meeting.

Accordingly, on the day designated the old gentleman rode up to brother Griffin's, leading a horse with a lady's saddle. The young lady was soon in the saddle, and she and her father were on their way to the meeting.

The next day I preached and gave the usual invitation to penitent believers to confess the Lord. The old gentleman who was sitting directly in front of the stand, arose instantly and came forward weeping, holding the same big cane in his hand. His daughter sprang to her feet, and uttering an exclamation of joy, rushed forward, and threw her arms around her father's neck and sunk down upon her knees by his side! It was a touching scene to see the father and his motherless daughter clasped in each other's arms weeping—the one shedding tears of bitter grief and penitence; the other tears of joy.

Had not the young lady resolutely obeyed the Lord, brooking the bitter opposition of her wicked father, both would doubtless have gone to perdition together; but now, hand in hand, they were treading the pilgrim's pathway to the city and home of God. It is always right for one to do his duty—to obey God. In such cases, all results well.

This touching story of conversion has been passed down for almost two hundred years and still touches the hearts of those who contend for the ancient gospel preached by Peter on the Day of Pentecost so long ago. Many gospel preachers have baptized individuals under the threat of bodily harm or death. Such was the case with B. F. Hall.

But think of the faith of the young girl. In spite of the promise of losing her home with the only family she had, she determined to give her life to Christ and obey His will in baptism. And if it had not been for her faith, her father would not have obeyed the gospel.

What a beautiful story! May we all "earnestly contend for the faith, once for all delivered unto the saints" (Jude 3).

Chapter 4

Gospel Meeting on Cypress Creek

As I tell this story of a Gospel Meeting on Cypress Creek that took place many years ago, I tell a story dear to my heart for two reasons. First, I live on Cypress Creek and for more than twenty years I have been able to open my back door and view this beautiful stream and listen to it as it flows past my home. It flows through Lauderdale County, Alabama, forming the western edge of the city of Florence, and then flows on into the Tennessee River about three miles south of my home. Second, this story is dear to my heart because of my love for the ancient gospel as it was preached on Cypress Creek many years ago.

There is historical significance to this gospel meeting. It was during this meeting that the first invitation song was known to have been sung, as those present were urged to obey a doctrine that had not been preached before in this area. That doctrine was the biblical doctrine of baptism for remission of sins, first preached on Pentecost in Acts 2:38.

The year was 1826. The gospel preacher in this meeting was Benjamin Franklin Hall, assisted by James E. Matthews. (It was early in the year 1826 that B. F. Hall, while visiting at Tompkinsville, Kentucky, read the Campbell—McCalla debate and came to the conclusion that baptism was necessary for the remission sins.)

From the viewpoint of many, the gospel meeting was a failure—only four young people responded to the gospel call. Three boys and a sixteen year old girl were baptized in the cold autumn waters of Cypress Creek.

But no one could ever imagine the significance of these conversions on a church that was trying to return to the Bible and restore New Testament Christianity according to principles set forth therein. Of the three boys, one of them was Alan Kendrick. Alan became a gospel preacher and baptized thousands, including his brother, Carroll Kendrick. Carroll Kendrick is believed to have baptized over 20,000 into Christ, and perhaps as many as 30,000, before laying down his armor and taking up his crown.

Another of the boys baptized in Cypress Creek at that meeting was Tolbert Fanning, described as a gangling youth "whose legs were too long for his britches." He was a giant of a man in his day and a giant in intellect and leadership as well. Fanning would leave Lauderdale County for Nashville and a college education. He became one of the leading agriculturists of the day, becoming the editor of the earliest agricultural journals.

Fanning also was a gospel preacher and a conservative during a time that liberal ideas had been filtering into the church. Fanning's most successful meeting took place in Russellville, Alabama in early 1842, when two-thirds of the heads of households in Russellville obeyed the gospel.

Tolbert Fanning's greatest influence was not as a preacher but as a teacher of preachers. By 1843, he had started a college on his farm near Nashville, Tennessee. He called this college "Elm Crag," and the name was later changed to Franklin College. (This farm is the present day site of the Nashville International Airport.) Here, Tolbert Fanning influenced young men who would become the leaders of the church for several generations. It was here that David Lipscomb, William Lipscomb, T. B. Larimore, and others were grounded in the faith, and it was David Lipscomb who led the fight against the missionary society and instrumental music in churches of Christ, keeping the churches of Christ from being swallowed up by the liberal movements of the day promoted by many churches and men of liberal persuasions. Indeed, the church of Christ owes a great debt to this man for helping preserve the truth of the gospel in the last century.

T. B. Larimore was influenced by Fanning at Franklin College and later moved to Florence, Alabama where he started his own college known as Mars Hill College. This college turned out hundreds of godly men and women who went forth proclaiming the gospel of Christ and living godly examples for others to imitate. By the turn of the twentieth century, T. B. Larimore was the most sought after gospel preacher on the planet, swamped with invitations to hold gospel meetings throughout the country. He converted several thousand to Christ.

An obituary in the Nashville Banner at the time of his death said that Larimore's accomplishments were like those of William Hayden, Walter Scott, Benjamin Franklin (who had baptized more than 10,000), and John Allen Gano (who had baptized approximately 10,000). The obituary made it plain that many believed T. B. Larimore had surpassed the accomplishments of these great men. In the life of T. B. Larimore, we see the influence of the boy with long legs and short britches who was baptized in that gospel meeting on Cypress Creek.

But what of the little sixteen year old girl who was baptized in Cypress Creek at that meeting in 1826? When she was ninety-eight years old, Sister Merriman was interviewed by C. E. Holt of Florence, Alabama. This would have been in the year 1908. Though some of her memories of that meeting on Cypress Creek had diminished (she thought the third boy baptized was Carroll Kendrick), when C. E. Holt asked about her conversion, Sister Merriman replied, "Oh, I was just a girl. I couldn't amount to anything like the others could. I raised fifteen children, though, and all of them members of the church."

Perhaps sister Merriman was the greatest of the converts at the Cypress Creek meeting, who labored without glory or renown, giving birth and raising children who would become Christians and they, in turn, raising their children to honor Christ and His gospel. Perhaps her influence has reached thousands over the years since her conversion.

James E. Matthews, the preacher who was with B. F. Hall in this meeting, was so impressed with Hall's sermon on the necessity of baptism for remission of sin that he wrote his old mentor, Barton Stone, several letters encouraging him to take this stand. (Hall, in his autobiography, said that when he asked Stone about baptism for remission of sins in 1826, Stone replied that he had preached it twenty-five years earlier, but that it was like pouring cold water on the listeners, and he quit preaching it.) Matthews' encouragement to Stone to take a position on baptism for remission of sins was successful, and this resulted in a unity meeting between the Stone and Campbell groups at the Hill Street Church in Lexington, Kentucky on January 1, 1832.

The meeting on Cypress Creek resulted in four young people being baptized, and as a result of the teaching of those young people, thousands obeyed the gospel. As a result of James Matthews' influence on Barton Stone to take the position that baptism was for remission of sins, those influenced by Stone and Campbell were united in this New Testament doctrine and began to work together to restore New Testament Christianity. This, too, resulted in thousands obeying the gospel.

The meeting on Cypress Creek was not a failure. In fact, there may never be such a wonderful meeting again on this side of eternity.

Chapter 5

Benjamin Lynn—A Man of Naïve Faith

A few years ago while researching restoration history in Versailles, Kentucky, I came across a document for which I had been searching, about a man named Benjamin Lynn, the man I believe to be the first gospel preacher in Alabama. The article, written and published in April 1946 in the *Filson Club Historical Quarterly*, gave a history of the life of Benjamin Lynn, one of the great explorers of Kentucky and a hero of the Revolutionary War. The article tells much of what a great woodsman Lynn was—how he lived among the Indians for several years and spoke their language and understood their ways. At length, the article tells of Lynn serving as a spy for General George Rogers Clark, brother of William Clark, famous as co-leader of the Lewis and Clark Expedition. The article tells of many of the battles Lynn had with the Indians in the early days of Kentucky.

Near the end of the Revolutionary War, Captain Benjamin Lynn became a Baptist preacher, but by about 1805 Lynn renounced the Baptist doctrine and decided to become a Christian only. Lynn sought baptism at the hands of Barton W. Stone, and he began to preach the simple gospel of Christ.

In the article published by the Filson Club, written by George and Helen Beattie, the authors made the following observation about Lynn:

> It is easy to understand how a man like Benjamin Linn (sic-Lynn), ignorant of theology and church doctrine, untrained in logic, and unaccustomed to critical thinking, would be bewildered by the arguments on the dogmas of Calvinism. The Bible was probably the only book he had ever read extensively and his study of it must have been

more of the heart than of the mind. Men of naïve faith like Linn (sic-Lynn) and his associates must have felt that such a church would be more like their Separate Baptist Church of earlier days than was the new United Baptist Church with its nearness to Calvinism.

Poor Benjamin Lynn! He was ignorant of theology and church doctrine and bewildered by arguments on the dogmas of Calvinism. Perhaps this reminds one of the Jewish leaders' perceptions of Peter and John. They thought they were "unlearned and ignorant men" (Acts 4:13).

These men were also considered unaccustomed to critical thinking. If only Lynn and others like him could have had a formal education with many books and sat at the feet of great theological scholars, might they have had a better understanding of the will of God? But all he had was the Bible, and so the Beatties concluded that Benjamin Lynn and his associates (i.e., those who held the same belief as Lynn) were poor simpletons, and were indeed *"men of naïve faith."* But alas, this naïve man influenced the spread of the gospel in at least six states.

One of the first men Lynn influenced to accept the simple gospel and become one of the men of "naïve faith," was John Mulkey of Tompkinsville, Kentucky. In his book, <u>Christians On The Oregon Trail</u>, Dr. Jerry Rushford tells that Benjamin Lynn and Lewis Byram "had a powerful impact on the thinking of a Baptist preacher named John Mulkey." In 1809, Mulkey led the majority of the Mill Creek Baptist Church away from the Stockton Valley Baptist Association in southern Kentucky. The Mill Creek church building, now known as "Old Mulkey," still stands and is preserved as an historical landmark by the state of Kentucky. Mulkey had a great influence in establishing churches in Southern Kentucky, Middle Tennessee, and Northern Alabama. Dr. Mansel Matthews, in a letter to David Lipscomb dated August 13, 1888, stated that he was baptized by John Mulkey in Spring Creek, Franklin County, Alabama, in

1823. This would be at the present day town of Tuscumbia, Alabama, now the county seat of Colbert County, Alabama. From this information we can see that Benjamin Lynn's influence was much greater than had been published previously.

Rushford goes on to point out that John Mulkey's son, Philip Mulkey, and John Mulkey's nephew, John F. Mulkey, were pioneers on the Oregon Trail, traveling to Oregon in 1853. Rushford says Philip Mulkey was by far the "most influential preacher arriving that fall." So Benjamin Lynn had an influence on the establishment of the church in Oregon through John Mulkey's son, Phillip.

Benjamin Lynn moved to Madison County, Alabama, in 1810. He began a church in Madison County and was buried in the churchyard in December 1814. He was sixty-five years old. His wife, Hannah Sovereigns Lynn, preceded him in death, having died in May of the same year. Two years later, his two daughters and their families moved to Lauderdale County, Alabama. His daughter, Rachel Lynn D'Spain and her family, settled at Waterloo in Western Lauderdale County. Rachel's son, Benjamin Lynn D'Spain (named for his grandfather, Benjamin Lynn), was a great gospel preacher of the 19th century, as was his son Alonzo Lynn D'Spain. Benjamin Lynn D'Spain, along with Dr. Mansel Matthews and David Crockett, led many of the members of the church of Christ at Waterloo, Alabama, to Texas in 1835. They became the first church of Christ in Texas. After Benjamin Lynn D'Spain led the church to Texas, he went to Mississippi and preached there. Later he went to Kentucky and finally settled in Texas.

Benjamin Lynn D'Spain's sister, Hettie Esther D'Spain, married Joseph A. Clark. They were the parents of Addison and Randolph Clark. Addison and Randolph, with the help of their parents, started Add-Ran College, which eventually became Texas Christian University.

Benjamin Lynn's daughter, Esther Lynn Chisholm, and her family started the first church of Christ on Cypress

Creek, in Lauderdale County. Esther's daughter, Dorinda, married Dr. Benjamin Franklin Hall, one of the earliest preachers to preach baptism for remission of sins in this country. Hall learned this truth by reading the Campbell-McCalla debate and immediately made application of the arguments that Campbell used. Hall preached the sermon and extended the invitation to which Tolbert Fanning responded, requesting baptism for remission of sins. James Matthews, upon hearing this sermon by Hall, proceeded to write a series of letters to Barton Stone, eventually causing Stone to once again preach baptism for remission of sins.

Esther Lynn Chisholm is buried in Lauderdale County, Alabama, just north of Florence about four miles north of the Chisholm Highway/Cox Creek Parkway intersection and fifty yards west of Chisholm Highway.

In a letter written by John Chisholm to Mr. John Barbee, written from Florence, Alabama, March 10, 1848, Chisholm wrote of his father-in-law, "I feel under great obligation to you for the interest you have taken to do justice to the services of one of the best men of his day and time."

I am thankful to God for **"men of naïve faith,"** like Ben Lynn, who simply read the Bible and determined to do what it said, even though it caused the loss of many friendships on this earth. Ben Lynn may have been naïve by the theological standards of the world, but he was a giant among men in many ways. He was an explorer, adventurer, warrior, and gospel preacher, and his life influenced thousands to obey the gospel. A laborer indeed, he influenced the establishment of the church in Kentucky, Tennessee, Alabama, Mississippi, Texas, and Oregon.

Were these men who preached the ancient gospel without creed book or discipline book naïve? I think not. I agree with his son-in-law, John Chisholm, that Benjamin Lynn was "one of the best men of his day and time." May we all strive to be more naïve like these men!

Chapter 6

John Mulkey—Standing on the Bible Alone

John Mulkey was born in South Carolina, January 14, 1773, and began at an early age preaching the gospel that had been preached by his grandfather, Phillip Mulkey, a talented preacher. John's father, Jonathon, also a preacher, was described by Isaac T. Reneau as "one of the most eloquent, pious and virtuous Baptist preachers in the State." By the age of twenty (in 1793), John Mulkey had commenced preaching in East Tennessee and became a very popular Baptist preacher. In the same year, he married Elizabeth (Betsy) Hayes. John was ordained to the ministry by the Holston Association prior to 1796, and was among the first delegates to represent the Mill Creek congregation at the annual session of the Mero District in 1798.

John Mulkey

John made his way to Mill Creek from East Tennessee, traveling by the way of the Cumberland River, which is about eight miles east of Mill Creek, near present day Tompkinsville, Kentucky. John and Elizabeth raised a family of ten children at Mill Creek. Reneau said, "All of their sons, save one, became a gospel preacher. Two of them, Isaac and John Newton, went on to be outstanding proclaimers of the gospel."

At Mill Creek, John Mulkey became the minister of the Mill Creek Baptist Church. The oldest record of the church is dated September 11, 1798. The record says, "Church met at Harland's and after divine worship proceeded to business as follows: John and Nancy Compton joined by letter and Bartholomew Wood by living testimony." The second item of business saw, "John Mulkey and John Wood chosen delegates to the asso(ciation)." The next record of the church is dated October 13, 1798. The record states, "[The] church met at the meetinghouse and after divine worship proceeded to business," proving that a meetinghouse was being constructed and was completed between the September 11, 1798 business meeting and the October 13, 1798 business meeting. This building was not to last for long. It burned five years later in 1803.

A second building was constructed in 1804. The April 12, 1804 minutes of the Mill Creek church stated, "Appointed a committee of seven members, John Wood, Nathan Breed, James Harlin (sic), Ephraim Ellis, Francis Baxter, Joseph Guest and Thomas Sulivan, (sic) at this place on the 28th of this April to fix a plan for building a meeting house." The May 11, 1804 minutes reported "that the meeting house is to be 50 feet long, 30 wide, shingled with joint shingles, 5 windows and three doors. A man to be hired to build it and paid in trade by subscription." The work was carried out, and the meetinghouse was built. This is the building that stands today.

The earliest problem the church had to deal with was drunkenness. The minutes of the March 9, 1798 meeting stated that Hannah Penington (sic) (and) Susanah (sic) Cummings made a complaint against "Brother Enoch Job (Jobe) for being intoxicated with liquor and he (was) suspended from privileges." However, on June 8, 1799, we find that "Brother Enoch Jobe came forward and satisfaction being gained he was restored." On May 11, 1799, the church granted "a certificate to Brother Jno Mulkey in order for him to obtain (a) license to mary (sic)." In 1799, he made application in Barren County, Kentucky for a license to perform marriages. According to the *Pioneer Baptist Church Records of South-Central Kentucky and the Upper Cumberland of Tennessee 1799-1899* by C. P. Cawthorn & N. L. Warnell, Mulkey was granted the license to perform marriages. It stated: "On motion of John Mulkey licens (sic) is granted him to Solemnize the rites of Marriage agreeable to Law he having produced credentials of his Ordination & of his being in regular Communication with the United Baptist Church and made Oath according to Law."

The church at Mill Creek had elders according to the New Testament pattern. On January 2, 1799, John Wood was appointed as an elder, and in the May 1800 record, Benjamin Gist was called to the office of "elder in this church, having been previously ordained." The same record says that Philip Mulkey and Josh Gist were "to be set about to the office of deacon by ordination."

The Mill Creek Baptist Church records, which are available on microfilm at the Southern Baptist Historical Library and Archives in Nashville, Tennessee, are informative. There are many cases of fellowship being withdrawn for various sins. For example, in August 1800, John Maddox and wife were dismissed with no reason stated, but in September 1800, James Tedlock was "excommunicated for the sin of fornication." James Tedlock was "acquitted" on July 10, 1801 and was accepted into fellowship. But the same day, Edmund Wade was excluded for the "act of adultery." Over the next several years, the church record mentions several cases of marital infidelity and sexual sin—some restored to the church after confession of sin, others dismissed for failing to do so.

John Mulkey labored to build up the congregation, which eventually had perhaps over three hundred in attendance. The 1809 roll had 171 names. In some cases, this did not include the spouses' names and did not include the names of children. The first record of any financial support given to Mulkey was stated in the December 12, 1801 minutes that said, "The church agrees to make up some provisions such as corn and pork for the support of Brother John Mulkey."

The two great revivals at the turn of the century in Kentucky caused new winds of the ancient doctrine to blow across the land. Beginning in 1800 with the Red River Revival near Russellville, Kentucky, and in 1801 at Cane Ridge near Lexington, Kentucky, these revivals put mainline religions on guard that there were challenges to the man-made doctrines of the various denominations. Under attack was the old Calvinist Doctrine that had become so much a part of the majority of the denominations. Many ministers began to reject the old established tradition of being required to adhere to the Philadelphia Confession of Faith. The people were no longer satisfied with the doctrines of total depravity, irresistible grace, unconditional election, limited atonement, and preservation of the saints. New thinkers began to question whether they were, indeed, born in sin when the Bible stated that "sons shall not bear the iniquity of the father" (Ezekiel 18:20). Irresistible grace required that one have a "religious experience" in order to be saved, and the mourner's bench type of religion was the religion of the day, with sinners trying to find a sign of their salvation.

John, initially, was very much opposed to these new religious thoughts, but over time he began wrestling with these thoughts. The doctrine of going back to the Bible alone as a guide, promoted by Barton W. Stone, had reached the Stockton Valley Baptist Association. John Mulkey was invited to come to the Baptist church on Big Barron River (later called Gamaliel) to turn Lewis Byrum from his acceptance of Stone's views. It was Abner Hill who wrote Mulkey and asked him to come to Big Barrens to turn Byrum back to the Baptists. Hill would later become a gospel preacher after the New Testament order and had a positive influence preaching the gospel in Alabama and Tennessee. (It was the preaching of Abner Hill that convinced a young W. D. Carnes to accept the gospel. Carnes became the president of the State College of Tennessee at Knoxville, now the University of Tennessee. He was also president of Franklin College near Nashville, Tennessee, Burritt College at Spencer, Tennessee, and Manchester College at Manchester, Tennessee. Educators seem to run in the Carnes family. James R. Cope, the great grandson of W. D. Carnes, was president of Florida College for many years. James

Cope's brother, Quill Cope, served as president of Middle Tennessee State University for several years.)

Mulkey began to consider the idea that one could be saved without any manmade confession, creed, discipline, or manual. At first, he rejected these new thoughts. Then he struggled with them. Finally, he embraced them, believing that man could be saved apart from any manmade doctrine and that salvation could be gained by standing on the Bible alone. Isaac T. Reneau wrote the following about Mulkey's break with the Baptists.

> In 1809, Mulkey was delivering a sermon on John 10 at the home of William Sims. While making a diligent effort 'to establish Calvinism,' his own argument convinced him that the doctrine was false. Being an honest and plain-spoken man, he expressed a change of conviction on unconditional election and other doctrinal matters.

The Calvinistic doctrine of unconditional election became a real concern for Mulkey. This doctrine held that God predetermined before time that certain ones would be saved (elected), others would be lost, and there was nothing the individual could do to change this. No doubt, Mulkey began to question why he should preach if certain ones would be saved and others lost, and his preaching would not change anything concerning the hearer's salvation.

In writing of this problem, Reneau wrote:

> A storm of controversy erupted in the Mill Creek Church and in the Stockton Valley Baptist Association. He (Mulkey) was charged with heresy and notified to stand trial at the August meeting of the Association. At that session, his opponents could not secure a guilty verdict. They called on five sister churches to assist them and scheduled another inquisition for October. After the charges were reiterated, they called for a show of hand, and the majority still favored Mulkey.

At the November session, the same accusations were received. Mulkey proposed that they 'drop all disputes and bear with one another,' but they replied, 'Never, till you come back to the very ground from which you started.' Mulkey then proposed to dissolve the Mill Creek Church which was unanimously accepted.

The record book of the Mill Creek Baptist Church contained this entry for the second Saturday in November 1809: "Church met and a decision took place and those whose names are above written declared that they would no longer remain under the constitution of the church and withdrawd (sic) from us consequently are no more of us."

The Mill Creek Baptist Church had been experiencing difficulties over the preacher, John Mulkey, for some time and the problem came to a head in late summer of 1809. The August 1809 record of the church stated: "Charges constituted against Brother John Mulkey in consequence of which the church agrees to send for help to assist us at our October meeting."

Isaac T. Reneau stated in Mulkey's obituary that the church agreed to call on five sister churches to help assist them with the problem they were having with Brother Mulkey. However, this is not mentioned in the minutes of the Mill Creek Baptist Church. When time came for the October meeting, the problem over John Mulkey was still unresolved and was continued to the November meeting. The minutes of the church business meeting, dated the second Saturday October 1809, stated:

> Church met agreeably to appointment with the helps and proceeded to hear the charges again constituted against Brother John (Mulkey) with other charges of like nature and when again hearing the charges debated and debated, we then concluded that he denied the essential doctrine of the Gospel such as denying in our esteem that Jesus Christ satisfied the demands of Law and Justice for his

people and died as our surety or that any man is saved by the Righteousness of Jesus Christ imputed to them, also finely (finally) for treating the church with contempt and going away and leaving us in our unpleasant situation.

As with many church problems, the solution is not compromise but division. This was the case of the Mill Creek Church. On Saturday, November 18, 1809, John Mulkey stood at the pulpit on the north side of the Mill Creek Baptist Church. The die was cast. The division took place with Mulkey inviting those who favored his teaching to exit by the west door and those who wished to continue in Baptist Doctrine to exit the east door. The majority exited the door to the west. The building was retained by the majority. The Baptists moved about a half-mile east of the old Mill Creek building to the other side of Mill Creek and established the new Mill Creek Baptist Church. The old Mill Creek Baptist Church became known as "Old Mulkey."

In a paper by Clayton Gooden, found at the Disciples of Christ Historical Society, Nashville, Tennessee, Gooden wrote of the incident:

> 'Now all you who believe as I do, follow me out the west door.' The words reverberated through the rough-hewn beams of the Mill Creek Baptist Church. It was Saturday morning, November 18, 1809. The congregation of some two hundred had gathered for the last time; and the words of John Mulkey were like a broad axe splitting the timbers of the Baptist traditions from top to bottom. All across Kentucky, Ohio, Tennessee, and South Carolina there were rumblings of discontent. Congregations were declaring themselves 'separate' or simply 'Christian Churches.' The restoration plea was being heard throughout the Western Reserve. And fervent revivals brought thousands to a great awakening of religion on the American frontier.

John walked slowly to the right of the long pulpit that stood on the north side of the building. Approaching the low door at the west end of the church, he bent slightly to clear the lintel and stepped out into the crisp air of the autumn morning. A snow had fallen leaving the ground a deep rust sprinkled over with a fine covering of white that resembled sugar. Gusts of wind were now blowing the frozen granules across the wooded cemetery where several Revolutionary War veterans lay resting from their struggle to win their country's independence. John looked out across the rough hewn stones. He was trying to win some independence, too… He wondered if the price would be as dear.

Among those who chose to leave the Baptist church for the Bible only religion taught by Mulkey was Hannah Boone Pennington. Hannah was the sister of the famous Daniel Boone. Her first husband, Stewart Pennington, was a Kentucky pioneer and a companion of Daniel Boone in his early exploration of Kentucky. Stewart Pennington was killed by Indians. This writer recently met a descendant of Hannah Boone Pennington. Max Ray, Hannah's descendant, is a member of the Grandview Church of Christ in Tompkinsville, Kentucky.

Another somewhat famous member of the newly established congregation was Nathan Breed. Those who have followed Revolutionary War history are familiar with the great battle of Bunker Hill. The Battle of Bunker Hill was actually fought on Breed's Hill. Nathan Breed was the owner of the property. Both Hannah Boone Pennington and Nathan Breed are buried in the cemetery at the Old Mulkey meetinghouse.

After the division in the Mill Creek church, the Baptists continued to demand the preaching credentials of John Mulkey. On October 20, 1810, the church minutes stated: "Brethren Ezekiel Springer and Thos. Wiley appointed to visit Brother John Mulky (sic) and demand his credentials."

Mulkey refused to give up his credentials and again on December 20, 1810, an attempt was made to secure Mulkey's preaching credentials. The minutes said: "Church met. The brethren that was (sic) appointed to demand brother John Mulky's credentials make report that he refused to give them up at the time."

There is no record of John Mulkey surrendering his preaching credentials to the Baptists. Perhaps he did at a later date.

There were others in South Central Kentucky preaching that people should return to the Bible alone for salvation and not put their hope in the doctrine of men. Among these were Rice Haggard and his brother, David, who lived in neighboring Cumberland County not far from Mulkey. Jerry Rushford, in his book, Christians on the Oregon Trail, said that Benjamin Lynn and Lewis Byram "were having a powerful impact on the thinking of a Baptist preacher named John Mulkey."

Benjamin Lynn, of Harrodsburg, Kentucky, had been a Baptist preacher and had experienced the same struggles of conscience that Mulkey was experiencing. By 1805, Lynn had determined to leave the Baptists to preach New Testament Christianity without the shackles of human creeds. He studied his Bible and came to the conclusion that he needed to be baptized for remission of sins. He knew of Barton Stone and his work at Cane Ridge, Kentucky, and Lynn walked from Harrodsburg to Cane Ridge to ask Stone to baptize him. Because Mulkey was experiencing the same struggle, Lynn was an important influence on Mulkey. About the time of the division in the Mill Creek Baptist Church (November 1809), Lynn's sons-in-laws, John Chisholm, Jr. and Marshall D'Spain, were in Alabama buying property in Madison County, with plans to move their families to Alabama, as well as their wives' parents, Benjamin and Hannah Sovereigns Lynn. Lynn established a church in Madison County, Alabama in 1810, which was, perhaps, the first Christian Church in Alabama. He and his wife died in 1814, and were buried in the church graveyard. The site of this building is unknown as well as the graves of Benjamin and Hannah Lynn. The Lynn's daughters, Esther Chisholm and Rachel D'Spain, and their families left Madison County, Alabama, in 1816, and moved to the newly opened Indian lands of Lauderdale County, Alabama, in the northwestern corner of the state. The Chisholm's started a congregation on Cypress Creek. The church is one of the oldest continually meeting churches in Alabama. Today it is known as the Stoney Point Church of Christ. The D'Spains' moved to western Lauderdale County and settled in the community of Waterloo where they established a church. This church continued to meet and grow at Waterloo until the fall of 1834, when most of them migrated to Texas and became the first church of Christ in Texas. This church was probably a large congregation, because they ordered three hundred song books from Barton W. Stone in 1832. Stone wrote, "Also, we have sent 300 Hymn Books to Waterloo, Alabama, consigned to James Witherspoon for Elders James E. and Mansel Matthews of Barton's, Lauderdale co. Alabama" (*Christian Messenger*, p. 380, 1832). The church members settled at Melrose, Texas, a few miles south of present day Nacogdoches, Texas. One of the leaders of this group was Benjamin Lynn D'Spain, the grandson of Benjamin Lynn. Benjamin Lynn D'Spain was a well-known gospel preacher, as was his son, Alonzo Lynn D'Spain.

John Mulkey continued with the Mill Creek church for several years, but he was in demand in other areas as well. In 1823, he held a meeting in Tuscumbia, Alabama. His old friend, Abner Hill, who had tried to sway John back to the Baptist, had become a gospel preacher and was living in Tuscumbia. It is probably through this connection that Mulkey came to Tuscumbia. Not much is known of this meeting, except that he baptized Mansel Matthews in Spring Creek. Many years later, Matthews would recall his baptism at the hands of John Mulkey in a letter to the *Gospel Advocate* (*GA*, August 22, 1888). Mansel Matthews became a medical doctor and gospel preacher. It was Matthews, along with Benjamin Lynn D'Spain, who led the church from Waterloo, Alabama, to Texas. David Crockett, who lived in Middle Tennessee near where Matthews preached, was persuaded to serve as a guide for this church, and he agreed to lead them to Texas. However, Crockett, in a hurry to get to the war in Texas, left the church in Memphis, and arrived at the Alamo in March 1835 and was killed. Matthews continued to preach in Texas until his death in 1891. His influence and conversion of perhaps thousands is a result of the truth that he learned from John Mulkey.

In 1825, John Mulkey moved his family to McMinn County in Southeast Tennessee. In a paper by John Waddey, titled *John Mulkey—Early Pioneer Preacher in McMinn County,* he states:

> Isaac Newton Jones knew John Mulkey well when he was a boy in McMinn County. He wrote a candid description of our subject in 1897. 'Old John Mulkey, as he was then called, was of medium height and slightly corpulent, weighing, I suppose, one hundred and eighty to two hundred pounds. He was a graceful horseback rider...Though he was not a rigid logician, his musical voice, aided by ideality, sublimity, and an easy-flow of language, readily fixed the attention of an audience; and when desirable, he could carry away his hearers by a whirlwind of natural eloquence.

Waddey goes on to write:

> John Mulkey's success in refuting the doctrines of the various denominations, putting their preaching champions to flight and winning their members over to the truth infuriated his sectarian neighbors. On one occasion, some of the more belligerent of them posted a sign on a tree in the forks of a road in McMinn County that offered 'twenty dollars reward for any man or set of men that will whip old John Mulkey and Rees Jones.' Such threats did not intimidate or deter

him from his mission. He was thoroughly prepared to endure hardness as a good soldier of Christ Jesus.

While in McMinn County, Mulkey wrote his old friend, Barton Stone, about a successful meeting in McMinn County. Stone quotes from Mulkey saying, "A letter under the date 9th Sept. from Eld. J. Mulky (sic) at Meesville, Tenn—informs us, that he has immersed between 30 and 40 persons since his last. May the Lord speed the labors of our beloved brother in the Lord" (*Christian Messenger*, vol. 8, 1834, p. 318). This was not the first letter to Stone concerning his work, nor would it be his last. Six years earlier, in 1828, Abner Hill wrote Stone, "I have had the satisfaction of being with the following preachers of the Gospel: John Mulkey, Phil. Mulkey, Elihu Randolph, Wm. D. Carns (sic), and brother Hobbs." Hill then pleads with Stone to deal with the subject of baptism for remission of sins. He wrote:

> Some of the brethren believe and preach that for a soul to believe and repent and be baptized for the forgiveness of sins, is the gospel plan for entering into the kingdom of Christ; others oppose this idea. This is a subject of great importance. I wish you would embrace the subject in a plain, forcible manner. This, no doubt, would have weight with the readers of the Christian Messenger" (*Christian Messenger*, vol. 3, 1828, pp. 42-43).

Interestingly, the next year, beginning in April 1829, Stone published three articles on the subject of baptism for the remission of sins written by James E. Matthews of Lauderdale County, Alabama. It is believed that these articles caused Stone to reevaluate his middle-of-the-road position on the necessity of baptism, and by 1832 he had once again begun to preach what he had preached twenty-five years earlier—the necessity of baptism for the remission of sins. This led to the union of the Campbell and Stone groups in January 1832.

While in McMinn County, John Mulkey became associated with Elihu and Robert Randolph. According to Larry Whitehead, editor of the *Alabama Restoration Journal*, Elihu and Robert were brothers of Elisha Randolph. Robert and Elihu worked with Elisha in Morgan County, Alabama, in the early 1820s. About 1832, Elisha moved to Blount County, Alabama and started the church on Lacon Mountain. About ten years later, he moved to Fayette County, Alabama, and was buried near his home in Fayette County.

According to the *Christian Messenger*, November 25, 1826, Robert and Elisha Randolph had attended a conference the previous August in Murfreesboro, Tennessee. Also in attendance were a number of gospel preachers, including Ephraim D. Moore, B. F. Hall, Abner Hill, James E. Matthews, Elisha Price, Wm. D. Carnes, and John and Phillip Mulkey.

Mulkey traveled throughout lower east Tennessee and worked in North Alabama. The legacy of John Mulkey extends far from the area of South Central Kentucky. His preaching would plant the seeds of New Testament Christianity in many states, including Tennessee, Alabama, Texas, and Oregon.

Jerry Rushford's book, Christians on the Oregon Trail, tells of the influence of John Mulkey in Kentucky and Oregon. Rushford holds Mulkey in esteem as a pioneer of the gospel in Kentucky. However, John Mulkey's influence on the church in Oregon was perhaps greater. John Mulkey's son, Phillip Mulkey, moved to Oregon, arriving there in 1853. He and his son, John F. Mulkey, were preachers in Oregon. Philip Mulkey's nephew, Isaac Newton Mulkey, arrived in Oregon in 1871. Three Mulkey brothers, nephews of John Mulkey, headed for Oregon in 1847. Thomas Mulkey died of "Mountain Fever" before reaching Oregon, but his brothers, Luke and Johnson Mulkey, arrived in Oregon and were staunch members of the church.

John Mulkey not only influenced his family to obey the truth, but also many of his family became preachers of the gospel. Mulkey had a great impact on others as well. One of these men, James McBride, formally a Baptist preacher in Kentucky and a member of the Stockton Valley Baptist Association, was influenced by Mulkey to leave the Baptist church. (Within two and a half years, more than half of the preachers of the Stockton Valley Baptist Association left to preach only the Bible.) In 1847, Dr. James McBride and his son, Thomas McBride, migrated to Oregon and had a great work in preaching the gospel.

John returned to Kentucky and lived there in his later years, dying at his farm near Tompkinsville. The obituary of John Mulkey was printed in the *Millennial Harbinger* and in the *Christian Review*, May 1845. Isaac T. Reneau concluded the obituary:

> John Mulkey spent the most of his time in preaching till about three years ago, when his health became so precarious that he was compelled to desist. The last year he was confined to his home, and the delightful company of his intelligent, pious and virtuous wife. He frequently and freely conversed with her on the subject of his "Departure for the land of rest," as he called it. Told her he had not dreaded death since he became a Christian; but that he was more than ordinarily willing to change worlds at this time. And to one of the elders he said—"You cannot think how willing I am to die!" Some days previous to his "departure," he requested his beloved to have two of his most favorite pieces sung while he should be dying; the one beginning "Jesus, thou art the sinner's friend"—the other, "The angels that watch'd round the tomb." But when his final dissolution came on, the friends were so immersed in grief for the dying father, saint, evangelist, that they could not sing. So in the midst of children, grandchildren, brethren, and weeping friends, he calmly fell asleep in Jesus—Dec. 13, 1844—15 m. before 1 o'clock, A. M. Father Mulkey delivered, in 51 years, upwards of 10,000 discourses himself, and left two sons eminent preachers, and a grandson just

commencing. Will they imitate his noble example? That they, and many more, may imitate it, is the prayer of this writer, ISAAC T. RENEAU.

The church at "Old Mulkey," as it was called, continued to meet until the 1830s. At that time, services were moved to private homes and to the Tompkinsville Courthouse where the church met for several years. In the early 1870s, a building for the Tompkinsville Church of Christ was planned. On November 16, 1871, two acres of land were purchased from Jefferson Gee for two hundred dollars. In 1872, the meetinghouse was constructed in downtown Tompkinsville. This building was replaced in 1932 by a new building that is still in use today.

After the church quit meeting at "Old Mulkey," the building fell into disrepair. In the 1890s, Winfield Emmert began an effort to restore the old church building. For awhile, the building was used for special services and other meetings, but over time, fell into disrepair once again. In the 1920s, there was a renewed interest in the "Old Mulkey" building, and local citizens contributed funds, supplies, and labor to repair the building and clean up the grounds.

Old Mulkey, built 1804

In 1931, the meetinghouse and grounds became a part of the Kentucky Department of Parks. It is the only state park dedicated to preserving a religious site in Kentucky. In 1995-1996, another restoration of the building took place, removing rotten logs and raising the church building to add a stone foundation to eliminate similar problems in the future. The chinking between the logs was also replaced. Today, the meetinghouse is used for special services, meetings, weddings, and family reunions celebrating their heritage. Over 40,000 individuals visit the site annually.

Chapter 7

The Carriage That Converted a Town

Tolbert Fanning

Tolbert Fanning was a well-known gospel preacher of the nineteenth century. He was born in Cannon County, Tennessee, in 1810. When he was eight years old, his family moved to Lauderdale County, Alabama, a portion of Alabama newly opened by the federal government as a result of a peace treaty with the Chickasaw Indians in 1816. Tolbert's father was a farmer, the main crop being cotton. Young Tolbert Fanning was brought up in the cotton field and developed a love for agriculture from an early age. By the time he was ten years old, he had read the Bible. Fanning was a tall youth who grew to be six feet, six inches in height. He was described as a boy "too tall for his britches." When sixteen years of age, he began to pay attention to the preaching of Ephraim D. Moore and James E. Matthews, who called themselves Christian preachers and were great and good men. From their teaching, he was encouraged to read the New Testament, with the view of really acquiring spiritual light. Soon all was plain, and his gloomy doubts gave place to an intelligent faith in the Lord Jesus Christ.

In November, 1831, he entered the Nashville University and was graduated in 1835. In 1843, he began to build Franklin College, and in October 1844, when the buildings were completed, Fanning was elected the first president. Fanning's conservative influence on young men like David Lipscomb, and T. B. Larimore, was perhaps the most stabilizing factor in churches of Christ that did not use the instrument and did not support the missionary society.

In his book, The Hazard of the Die, James Wilburn relates a story about Tolbert Fanning on one of his tours. The story tells how a broken spring on Fanning's carriage caused him to return to a town to preach. Ironically, that same town on the previous night had shown so much prejudice that Fanning had determined to leave.

Fanning left Nashville in January 1842, his destination being Columbus, Mississippi. He decided he would travel to Florence, Alabama, to visit his old home place. He did so and continued on to Tuscumbia, Alabama, where he preached at the Tuscumbia church of Christ. From Tuscumbia, Fanning with his wife, Charlotte, continued to Russellville, Alabama, about fifteen miles away. Stopping over in Russellville, Fanning decided to hold worship services and preach at "candle lighting." Fanning had little success, found the people of Russellville to be prejudiced against the gospel and decide that he would leave the next day. Notice Wilburn's description of what was to follow:

> That first night, Fanning spoke to a small audience on, 'The Importance of Searching the Scriptures.' Among the three hundred people in the community he found so much prejudice that he climbed into his carriage the very next morning, convinced that his time would be spent better somewhere else.
>
> With Jacob Faithful (Fanning's horse) heading south toward Columbus, Mississippi, they struggled along through the mud. But when they had gone less than a mile one of the springs on the carriage broke. Together, Charlotte and Tolbert trudged through the mud back to Russellville to investigate the possibilities for having it repaired.
>
> When they learned that they would have to wait several days until a part could be shipped from another city, Fanning announced around town that there would be preaching each evening at candle lighting. Then he

set out to visit the farmers and find out more about their agricultural pursuits.

Perhaps it was largely a credit to Fanning's ability to mingle with the people and intelligently discuss their farming interests that their prejudice began to subside and the number who came to hear him preach began to grow. By the time that the carriage was repaired, about forty people had been baptized, and Fanning couldn't leave.

Within a month, Fanning had baptized over one hundred persons. When he finally decided to continue his tour, leaving a town where he had found little interest and great prejudice, Fanning was able to leave a congregation consisting of more than two-thirds of the heads of the families in the community! He would never declare that God broke his carriage spring though he occasionally mused that the salvation of precious souls often depends upon what, to us, seems to be a very small matter.

Dr. Samuel Sevier, son of John Sevier, former Governor of Tennessee, was one of five Christians in Russellville at the time, and the only male Christian. This immediate growth in the church in Russellville must have been a great joy to Samuel Sevier. Dr. Sevier's obituary in the *Millennial Harbinger* in 1850, states that Dr. Sevier had been associated with the Christian church since 1825, and "he became instrumental in the conversion of many souls to God."

What if the spring on the carriage had not been broken? One can only guess that it would be many years before the church was established in Russellville, Alabama. Today, many members of churches of Christ are found in Russellville and Franklin County, Alabama because of Fanning's influence.

Chapter 8

Baptism without Consent

"Raccoon" John Smith (1784-1868) was one of the more colorful characters of the restoration movement. His quick wit and quick verbal exchange, along with his ability to relate to the common people, made him a favorite among the people of Kentucky where he spent most of his life. His nickname, "Raccoon," was the result of being asked to preach and he began by introducing himself as John Smith from Stockton Valley. He said, "Down there saltpeter caves abound and raccoons make their homes." Coming from an area where raccoons abounded, John became known far and wide as "Raccoon" John Smith.

John Smith

Born in East Tennessee, he was raised in the Stockton Valley area of South Central Kentucky. The son of strong Calvinistic Baptists, he desired to preach but was condemned by other preachers because he had never "received the call to preach."

In 1814, John sold his farm in Kentucky and moved to Madison County, Alabama, to take advantage of cheap land that had recently become available. In January, 1815, while away from home, his cabin caught fire and two of his children, Eli and Elvira, burned to death. His wife, Rebecca, refused to be comforted and never recovered from her broken heart. John Augustus Williams in his biography of Smith titled <u>Life of Elder John Smith</u> recorded the decline of Rebecca Smith:

> But the pale, melancholy face of that wife never brightened again. His own sunny temper could not

remove the shadow from her brow. As soon almost as she was comfortably housed in her new cabin, the good woman sickened and died, and they buried her by the ashes of her children.

Smith lost most of his material wealth in the fire, and almost immediately following his wife's death, became ill with what was diagnosed as the "Cold Plague." For three months, Smith was near death. Finally, he regained his strength and shortly after returned to Kentucky.

Smith continued his interest in preaching and became acquainted with the work of Alexander Campbell through Campbell's paper *The Christian Baptist*. When Campbell made a preaching trip to Kentucky, Smith was determined to hear him speak. Campbell was scheduled to speak at Flemingsburg, twenty miles from Smith's home at Mt. Sterling, Kentucky. Smith rode with Billy Vaughn to hear Campbell speak. Campbell spoke on Galatians 4, and Smith became so enthralled with the great message Campbell delivered, he felt cheated that he had ridden twenty miles to hear Campbell speak for such a short time. Williams tells the story of Smith's ride home and the discussion he had with Billy Vaughn:

> "Is it not hard, Brother Billy, to ride twenty miles, as I have done, just to hear a man preach thirty minutes?"
> "You are mistaken, Brother John. Look at your watch. It has surely been longer than that?" He looked at his watch, and, to his surprise, saw that the discourse had been just two hours and a half long. Holding up his watch, he remarked:
> "I have never been more deceived. Two hours of my life are gone, I know not how, though wide awake, too, all the time!"
> "Did you find out, Brother John," now asked Vaughn, 'whether he was a Calvinist or an Arminian (sic)?'"

> "No," replied Smith, "I know nothing about the man; but be he saint or devil, he has thrown more light on that epistle, and on the whole Scriptures, than I have received in all the sermons that I have ever heard before." (Williams, pp. 139-140)

Shortly after this, Smith had the opportunity to meet with Campbell, and discuss religion with him. Smith became convinced that Campbell preached the truth presented in the New Testament, and became determined to preach the Bible and the Bible alone, free from the creeds of men and especially the Calvinistic Doctrine that he had espoused most of his life.

A plain man, with little education, Smith was able to talk to people about religion and to show them the Bible truths. Campbell said of Smith, "John Smith is the only man I ever knew who would have been spoiled by a college education." With little formal education, Smith memorized much of the scripture and freely quoted from it. His Bible knowledge and good-natured disposition made him a favorite of the people.

There are many amusing incidents in the life and work of John Smith. In Louis Cochran's classic restoration novel, <u>Raccoon John Smith</u>, Cochran relates a story about Smith as he was riding past a Methodist camp meeting one day. Smith observed a rebellious infant being sprinkled. The baby squirmed and resisted, but to no avail. The infant was baptized according to the Methodist Discipline. Cochran relates that Smith dismounted his horse and grabbed the Methodist preacher by the arm and attempted to lead him toward the creek a few yards away.

> "What are you trying to do, Brother Smith:" the young preacher protested. "Are you out of your mind?"
>
> "What am I trying to do?" John affected deep surprise. "Why, sir I am going to baptize you by immersion into the death, burial, and resurrection of

our Lord Jesus Christ, according to his commandment."

"But I have no desire for such baptism. I know of you; you are called 'The Dipper.' But you are not going to dip me. I'm a Methodist; let me go!"

John tightened his hold on the man's arm while the crowd watched, some in apprehension, others in amusement. "That is a scoffer's blasphemy of a holy ordinance," he said sternly. "Are you a believer?"

"Of course I'm a believer," the preacher said indignantly. "But I'm not willing to be immersed. It would do no good for you to baptize me against my will. It would be wrong!"

"I don't understand," John said. Only a few minutes ago you baptized a helpless baby against its will, although it screamed and kicked. Did you get its consent first: Come along, sir, we will have no more of this foolishness."

The crowd broke into open laughter, and John gave the young preacher a quick pull toward the creek, and then as suddenly released him. He waved to the people for silence.

Brethren and friends, I shall be in the neighborhood for a little while visiting among you; let me know if this poor, misguided man ever again baptized another without his consent. For you have heard him say that it would do no good, that it would be wrong (Cochran, pp. 324-325).

Cochran writes that Smith spoke to the crowd for almost an hour and the people listened closely. He pointed out the gospel plan of salvation. When John Smith extended the invitation, seven young people, all from Methodist families responded, requesting baptism by immersion. He led them to the creek and baptized them. As he stepped back on the bank, the mother of one of those baptized, confronted him. "You are a demon," she cried. "When you led my innocent young daughter into that water, you led her that much further toward hell."

Raccoon John was much shocked and surprised by the statement; but then replied, "My good sister," he said quietly, "When you read your Bible more and your Methodist discipline less, you will learn that people do not go to that place by water."

Cochran says in his account of this incident that Smith used the following passage in his sermon: "Or do you not know that as many of us as were baptized into Christ Jesus were baptized into His death? Therefore we were buried with Him through baptism into death, that just as Christ was raised from the dead by the glory of the Father, even so we also should walk in newness of life" (Romans 6:3-4).

Chapter 9

Raccoon John Smith and the Campbellites

In 1834, the venerable "Raccoon" John Smith made a preaching trip to Madison County, Alabama. John Augustus Williams, in his book, <u>Life of Elder John Smith,</u> relates an incident about Smith as he traveled from Mount Sterling, Kentucky, to Huntsville, Alabama. Smith stopped to eat breakfast one morning at an inn in Sparta, Tennessee. The landlady received him politely and prepared his breakfast. A conversation with the lady commenced. She, upon finding out where Smith was from, said that she had heard from travelers of a strange sort of people up in Kentucky called Campbellites, and asked Smith about them. Williams records the following dialogue:

> "Yes, madam," replied he, "there are some in my own, neighborhood."
> "You have seen some of them then?" said she.
> "Yes, madam, but they don't like that name."
> "Well, how do they look?" said she. "Do tell me, sir."
> "Those I have seen look pretty much like other people."
> "I would really like to see one, so much," said she, musingly; "I'd give more to see one of those people than any show. I'm told that when anybody wants to join them, they just put them under the water, and then let them go. One man told me that they would sometimes take people by force, and drag them down into the water; that they even chased after people, and ran them down; that they once took a fancy to a poor fellow, and ran him five miles before they caught him, and then, after putting him in, they just left him there to get home, or to heaven, the best way he could."

"That was a very long-winded fellow, ma'am," interrupted Smith, to run five miles before the Campbellites caught him.'"

"I don't know what I wouldn't give to see one of them," said she, pouring out a cup of coffee, and handing it to her guest, who had taken his seat at the table with far more appetite than humor.

"How do you think a Campbellite would look?" inquired Smith, after breaking his fast a little.

"Well," said she, "I imagine they have a sort of wild, fierce, fanatical look about them."

"I think I can manage for you to see one," said Smith, as he received his second cup from her hands.

"I'd give any thing (sic) almost, if you would, sir," said the lady.

"Madam," said he, laying down the knife and fork which he had plied with more than usual assiduity, and raising his bland, good-natured face upon her, "look right at me, and you will see one! But don't be afraid," continued he, seeing her start, and then blush with confusion, "I am a civil Campbellite, and will not chase you into the water."

Having finished his meal, he withdrew from the table, and re-assuring her of his perfectly civil disposition, requested her to take a seat and listen to what he had to say about those singular people. He told her what they believed and preached, and corrected all the wicked stories that had been told against them (Williams, Life of Elder John Smith, pp. 400-401)!

Chapter 10

The Old Upping Stone

For most of the people who were born in the twentieth century and are still living, the memory of primitive conditions of days gone by is faded or non-existent. Most people today do not remember going to the outhouse, cooking over a wood stove, riding in a horse drawn wagon, or walking to town. Most cannot imagine cutting a tree with an axe or building a house without a circular saw. Times have changed and with it the memory of many everyday things of previous centuries.

With the advent of the automobile, the days of conveyance by animal power came to an abrupt halt. As automobiles became more dependable, even people in rural areas began to depend more and more on mechanized transportation and equipment. Soon the oxcart and horse drawn wagon, carriage, and surrey were replaced. With these passing antiques, another item of daily use in the olden days was lost to remembrance by succeeding generations. This item was the upping stone. It was also called, upping rock, upping block, leaping block, leaping stock, and jossing block. All of these terms refer to the same item—an item of convenience a century ago. These stones graced courthouse lawns, business establishments, city streets, churchyards, and homes.

The upping stone was used to "step on" to mount or dismount horses, wagons, carriages, etc. Many times the conveyance stood three feet from the ground, and that first step was a giant one. As people today pull their vehicles under the "drive through" at the church building to conveniently unload passengers, in years gone by, carriages, wagons, and people on horseback would line up in the churchyard at the old upping stone. Children were often handed down, while the ladies would gingerly step from the conveyance to the upping stone to dismount. The reverse process was in order after services.

If only these stones could talk. They could tell of life a century ago. They could tell of the things that went on around them. They could speak of the children playing on them. They could speak of ladies with multiple petticoats and fashionable shoes gently stepping on them as they dismounted. They could tell of the rough boots of a man accustomed to working in the fields, grinding his hob-nailed heel across the stone as he attempted to mount his horse.

The churchyard upping stones could tell of gospel meetings gone by, of all day singings, and dinner on the ground. They could tell of the children running and playing in the churchyard. They could tell of funerals held in the building and of drab dressed mourners with tears streaming as they walked to a nearby cemetery to bury a loved one. If they could smell, they could tell of the smell of animals and the smell of sturdy leather leads, straps, and saddles made for the animals that stood nearby. They could tell of the smell from nearby farms and of the smoke from tobacco, being smoked by men in the churchyard. If they could hear, they could tell of thousands of sermons, songs, and prayers they had heard. They could tell of being watered down by a preacher and new convert as they returned from a nearby stream or pond where a baptism had taken place, now returning on their way to the building to find privacy to change their wet clothes.

Rock Creek Church

The old upping stones could tell of the glory of the changing season, of being covered with snow in the winter, and of the beauty of spring and trees and plants springing to life around it. The upping stones could tell of the heat of summer and of wagons gently rolling by to the store or to the fields. They could tell of the glorious colors of fall as leaves gently fell around the stone forming a soft carpet.

One old upping stone that is still around today is the upping stone of the Rock Creek Church of Christ located in rural Colbert County, Alabama. This upping stone is perhaps one-hundred-fifty years old. It stood in the churchyard for many years, and if seeing, would have seen men like T. B. Larimore, John Taylor, and the Srygley family (who lived close enough to walk to the building) who produced two nationally known gospel preachers, Fletcher Douglas Srygley and Filo Bunyon Srygley.

Some time ago, this writer saw a brother in Christ who had lived in the Rock Creek area all his life. When asked if he remembered the old upping stone, Hershel Henry replied, "I sure do." He told of having two steers that were broke to a yoke. He said, "When I was a boy I would ride an old steer to the church and use the upping stone to dismount from the steer." He said that the steer moved slowly, but it beat walking. He also told of occasionally having the privilege of riding a horse to the church. He enjoyed the horse more because it was faster than the steer.

Rock Creek Church Upping Stone

The church at Rock Creek quit meeting in the 1960s and the property was sold. The new owner of the property, being afraid that the stone would "disappear," donated the stone to Heritage Christian University in Florence, Alabama, some thirty miles away. Wayne Kilpatrick, Professor of Church History at HCU, moved the stone from Rock Creek and placed it in a fitting memorial garden on the HCU campus. Even though moving the stone caused an uproar by those of the Rock Creek community, many felt for preservation purposes, moving the stone to the new location was best. The Rock Creek upping stone measures 21 inches by 22 inches at the base and is 29 inches tall. It has two steps, and weighs several hundred pounds.

Chapter 11

Emotionalism in Worship in the Nineteenth Century

Emotionalism as related to worship is much different from emotion. Emotion is a strong feeling, such as love, fear, anger, grief, joy, sorrow, etc. Emotionalism is guided by feeling rather than truth. It is the old "better felt than told" religion, where feeling and emotions trump logic and reasoning, and the feeling itself becomes the "evidence."

Cane Ridge Meeting-August 1801

Emotionalism in worship has been around for a long time. We will share two examples of this from the early 19th century. The "Great Awakening" of religious fervor was demonstrated in August 1801, when according to the estimate of Barton W. Stone, between twenty thousand to thirty thousand people showed up for a camp meeting at Cane Ridge, Kentucky. From Barton Stone's autobiography, Stone described the emotionalism that took place at Cane Ridge, and listed some of the "exercises," as he called them.

Falling Down- He said that often "the subject of this exercise would, generally, with a piercing scream, fall like a log on the floor, earth, or mud, and appear as dead." Stone said there were thousands of such cases.

The Jerks- Stone mentioned what he called the jerks, in which the subject would be affected and "jerk backward and forward, or from side to side, so quickly that the features of the face could not be distinguished." Stone said, "I have seen the person stand in one place, and jerk backward and forward in quick succession, their head nearly touching the floor behind and before." He said this exercise affected "all classes, saints and sinners, the strong as well as the weak."

Dancing- This "generally began with the jerks, and was peculiar to professors of religion. The subject, after jerking awhile, began to dance, and then the jerks would cease."

Barking Exercise- Stone said this exercise was given its name by "contemptuous opposers." He said it was nothing more than the jerks. He said one with the jerks "would often make a grunt, or bark…from the suddenness of the jerk."

Laughing Exercise- Stone said "it was a loud, hearty laughter but it did not excite laughter in others." He said it "excited solemnity in saints and sinners. It is truly indescribable."

Running Exercise- Stone said that the running exercise "was nothing more than, that persons feeling something of these bodily agitations, through fear, attempted to run away, and thus escape from them; but it commonly happened that they ran not far, before they fell, or became so greatly agitated that they could proceed no farther."

Singing Exercise- "The subject in a very happy state of mind, would sing most melodiously, not from the mouth or nose, but entirely in the breast, the sounds issuing thence." Stone said, "It was most heavenly" and "something surpassing anything we had known in nature."

While the logical mind has trouble explaining these "exercises," the emotional mind quickly attributed such things to a direct operation of the Holy Spirit, ushering in a "Great Awakening" of religion in a spiritually starved western frontier. However, Stone concludes this story by saying, "there were many eccentricities, and much fanaticism in this excitement." Fanaticism is defined as "irrational zeal." Irrational is the antithesis of the ability to reason or of being of a sound mind (American Heritage Dictionary).

Account of Benjamin Franklin Hall

One of the great preachers of the 19th century was Dr. B. F. Hall who lived in Lauderdale County, Alabama where he studied dentistry and married Dorinda Chisholm. Hall began preaching as a Baptist but learned the truth after reading the Campbell-McCalla debate in the year 1826. Hall, in his unpublished autobiography, tells of the general and accepted preaching style of the early 19th century. His was clearly an "emotional based" style of preaching.

> We were very zealous, and frequently spoke at the top of our voice, and sometimes screaming at such a rate as almost to split our throat. We substituted sound for sense, indeed, figuratively speaking, we supposed that the power was in the thunder instead of the lightening; hence we thundered more than we lightened or enlightened, for, in truth, we had not much light to emit.
> The religion of those days consisted principally of feeling; and those who shouted the loudest and made the greatest ado, were looked upon as the best Christians. Hence our preaching, our prayers, and songs we adapted to excite the emotions. We would clap and rub our hands, stamp with our feet, slain down and tear up the Bible, speak as loud as possible and scream at the top of our voice, to get up an excitement. I often blistered my hands by clapping and rubbing them together; and my feet were made sore by repeated stamping. My voice was clear, and its tones silvery. I could sing for hours without being tired or becoming hoarse. I was excitable, and dealt much in the pathetic. I was considered good at exhortation. Death, the judgment, heaven and hell, were my favorite themes. Here fancy had ample room for play; and on such themes the feelings of the masses could be reached. Knowing my forte, the brethren were want (sic) to have me to bring up the rear on occasions when an excitement was desired. I

frequently spoke when, on account of the loud shouting of Christians, and the screams of sinners, I could scarcely hear my own voice. Then was the time, after a short pause to call for mourners, and it was seldom they failed to come. I have known them to come in such numbers and crowd so closely around me as I stood before the stand, in the midst of the audience, that, when we were about to pray for them, I had not room to kneel down. Sometimes the excitement would be so great—so many brethren all praying aloud at once, and mourners screaming and begging for mercy, that no single voice could be distinguished from the rest. I have spent whole nights singing, praying and trying to instruct weeping, broken-hearted sinners how to 'get religion,' and, now and then rejoicing with one who had just 'got through.'

By his own account, Hall states that the purpose of his preaching, and the preaching of others, was to excite the emotions of the listeners. This was accomplished by loud preaching, clapping the hands, stamping the feet, being slain down, and tearing up Bibles. Hall even admitted that his favorite subjects were those where he could play on people's emotions—"Here fancy had ample room for play," he stated. Hall said that he was the "go to man" when "excitement was desired." Hall said all of this was for the purpose of "getting religion" and "getting through", both expressions of the "mourner bench" religion of the day, when one was believed to be saved through a "religious experience."

Exciting the emotions leaves much undone in the realm of logic and reasoning. In fact, as Hall later learned, this was contrary to the Bible. At Thessalonica, Paul "reasoned with them from the scriptures" (Acts 17:2); at Athens, "he reasoned in the synagogue with the Jews and with the Gentile worshipers, and in the marketplace daily with those who happened to be there" (Acts 17:17); at Corinth, "He reasoned in the synagogue every Sabbath, and persuaded both Jews and Greeks" (Acts 18:4); at Ephesus, "he went into the synagogue and spoke boldly for three months, reasoning and persuading concerning the things of the kingdom of God," and he was also "reasoning daily in the school of Tyrannus" (Acts 19:8-9).

Biblical preaching began as a persuasion through the use of logic and reasoning, moved on to persuasion through emotionalism, switched back to logic and reasoning, and is now manifested in an explosion of emotionalism. Experiences based solely on emotionalism and devoid of Biblical authority have become the norm in protestant churches during our time.

Can you picture the apostle Paul preaching in some churches today with a "rock concert" atmosphere? Can you see Paul trying to excite the crowd by using the techniques of today's preachers—techniques to arouse emotions that would cause people to forget the solemnity of worship to God. Would Paul devote himself to the exercise of an emotionally based religion?

When the validity of Christianity is based on emotionalism rather than knowledge of God's word, we find a system of religion in deep spiritual poverty. One writer said, "Emotion without truth produces empty frenzy and cultivates shallow people who refuse the discipline of rigorous thought."

Emotionalism in preaching reminds me of the preacher who wrote in his notes: "This point weak. Pound hard on podium."

Beware, brethren! "We are warming by the devil's campfire."

Chapter 12

Dr. Lewis Clark Chisholm

Chisholm

Dr. L. C. Chisholm was a faithful member of the church of Christ for over seventy years, and a century after his death, he serves as an example of a Christian gentleman—a man of high moral character and integrity. Chisholm was born in Tuscumbia, Alabama, on May 20, 1822, and died at the "ripe old age" of ninety-one years in Nashville, Tennessee, on December 3, 1913.

L. C. was the son of Gillington and Cynthia Hill Chisholm. Cynthia's brother was Abner Hill, a preacher who was associated with John Mulkey before Mulkey left the Baptists, and one of the preachers from the Stockton Valley (Kentucky) Baptist Association who left the Baptists to restore New Testament Christianity. Abner Hill was a Justice of the Peace in Tuscumbia in 1820 and probably arranged the first gospel meeting held in Franklin County (which at the time included Colbert County). The extent of the meeting is not known, but what is known is that John Mulkey came to Tuscumbia from Tompkinsville, Kentucky, and preached in this meeting. Mansel W. Matthews who was living in Lauderdale County, Alabama, at the time, was baptized in Spring Creek at Tuscumbia in this meeting in the year 1823. Matthews would spend the next seventy years preaching the gospel. Abner Hill relates in his autobiography that his brother-in-law, Gillington Chisholm, requested Hill to baptize him. A few years later in 1834, Dr. W. H. Wharton established the church in Tuscumbia. From early childhood, L. C. Chisholm had heard the ancient gospel preached many times.

Chisholm was baptized into Christ for the remission of sins during the great gospel meeting in Russellville, Alabama, in 1842, when Tolbert Fanning's preaching converted two-thirds of the households in Russellville. This great meeting in Russellville resulted in over one hundred obeying the gospel and a church being established.

The only male Christian in Russellville, Alabama, before Fanning's great meeting was Dr. Samuel Sevier, son of John Sevier, first governor of Tennessee. No doubt, as a result of the sharing of religious convictions between the Sevier family and the Chisholm family, three of Gillington Chisholm's children married three of the Dr. Samuel Sevier's children. L. C. Chisholm married Jane Sevier. Malinda Chisholm, married Archibald Sevier. Mary Chisholm married Dr. Daniel Vertner Sevier, a long time physician in Frankfort and Russellville, Alabama

Soon after L. C. was converted by Tolbert Fanning, he decided he would attend Fanning's college at Elm Crag (later to become Franklin College) where Fanning served as president. He did so in 1843 but only remained a short time, stating that Elm Crag did not suit his wants, and enrolled at the Old Lasea College, in Maury County, Tennessee, under the direction of John M. Barnes where he remained three years. He later pursued training in dentistry and became a very successful dentist in Tuscumbia, Alabama.

Chisholm did some preaching, but it seems that his preaching was infrequent. He is, however, listed as the preacher of the Russellville (Alabama) Church of Christ in 1849 by *The Yearbook of the Disciples*. During the time L. C. Chisholm was preaching in Russellville, his father-in-law, Dr. Samuel Sevier, died. Dr. Chisholm reported the death to Alexander Campbell, and Campbell published it in February 1850 on p. 114 of the *Millennial Harbinger*. It is obvious from his writing that Chisholm held his father-in-law in high regard. The following is part of the obituary that Chisholm wrote:

RUSSELVILLE, Ala., Nov. 17, 1849. Died, at his residence in Russelville (sic), Ala., on Thursday, October 25th, at 3 o'clock, Dr. SAMUEL SEVIER, (son of John Sevier, former Governor of Tennessee,) in the 65th year of his age, after an illness of several months, which he bore with calm and Christian resignation. He left, to lament the irreparable loss, an affectionate wife and eight children-four having gone before, and are doubtless with him in that house not made with hands, eternal in the heavens. He united with the Christian brethren in the year 1825, having been a member of the Methodist Episcopal Church some six years previous, and for twenty-four years of toil and care fought under the banner of Prince Emmanuel, bearing the persecution and scorn of wicked men for his name's sake.

He was a kind and affectionate husband; a pious and exemplary father. During the whole time of his affliction he ceased not to exhort his children to hold out faithful unto the end; and when death came, (for which he had so frequently prayed,) to relieve him from his sufferings, with a smile he folded his arms, commended his spirit to that God who gave it, and breathed his last. Thus he fought a good fight, finished his course, kept the faith, and henceforth there is laid up for him a crown of righteousness, which the Lord, the Righteous Judge, shall give at that day; and not to him only, but unto all them that love his appearing.

Dr. Chisholm's professional success translated to material wealth, and Chisholm became the owner of one of the most beautiful homes in Tuscumbia, Alabama. The home known as "Locust Hill" still stands today. Built in 1823 by Colonel William Winter, the house is described as "having fine proportions, great chimneys, and handmade-brick walls thirteen inches thick, windows with deep reveals, and charming woodwork." Chisholm bought the house prior to the Civil War.

On February 22, 1863, Union cavalry under command of Colonel Florence M. Cornyn attacked Tuscumbia, and Cornyn chose the home of Dr. L. C. Chisholm as his headquarters. From there, orders were given to wreak havoc on the town. Cornyn's 1,200 man brigade was dubbed the "Destroying Angels." Composed of units from Missouri and Ohio, they were joined by the 1st Alabama, USA, a unit of Southerners primarily from Winston County, Alabama, who refused to fight for the South and joined the Union Army.

Cornyn's men camped in Tuscumbia. They tore down fences belonging to private residences to use for firewood, and helped themselves to the contents of nearby homes, devastating the people of Tuscumbia. They carried off everything in the smoke houses. They also took all the flour, and other food items. The soldiers used shocking gestures and crude language toward the women. When complaints were made to Cornyn, he made it clear he did not care what his men did. Some of the citizens were required to pay ransom to keep their homes from being burned.

This was the man who made his headquarters in the home of Dr. L. C. Chisholm. This writer toured Locust Hill and the current owners, the Gilchrists, showed me their home. We were shown a bloody stain on the hardwood floor as one enters the parlor of the home. The blood evidently dried on the floor, staining the wood. Even after numerous cleanings over the past 150 years, the bloody footprint stain is still visible. The stain is an ever present reminder of injury and death that resulted from the Civil War. According to oral history, the home was used as a hospital for the wounded and many were cared for at the home. Probably, Dr. Chisholm's services were required to provide medical attention to the wounded. Perhaps Locust Hill remains today because of its use to the Union Army while in Tuscumbia.

Shortly after the atrocities in Tuscumbia, Dr. Chisholm's wife, Jane, died, and Dr. Chisholm moved his family to Nashville, Tennessee. There he became a neighbor and close friend of James E. Scobey, a gospel preacher and former professor at Franklin College. Dr. Chisholm also became closer to Tolbert Fanning, the man whose preaching converted him to Christ over twenty years earlier. When Scobey was making preparations to write his book, Franklin College and Its Influences, Scobey asked L. C. Chisholm to contribute to the book. The following are a few of Chisholm's comments about Fanning:

> With this long and intimate acquaintance, I can truly say that Tolbert Fanning had but few, if any, equals in his day. He was a strong man from every standpoint. As an educator, he had no peer in Tennessee. His work along that line gives ample proof of the fact. As a public speaker, his style was simply inimitable. His voice was strong, and his articulation was distinct. As a preacher, he was always logical and scriptural. He appealed to the common understanding of his audience, holding it spellbound to his subject. As a neighbor, he was kind and generous. He was energetic and pushing in all his business. In worship he was humble and fervent in spirit. But, like all Adam's race, he had his likes and dislikes, and made no pretensions to perfection. He loved the dog and the horse, and delighted in seeing them brought up to their highest capacity. For this he was often criticised (sic), even by his brethren, and often maligned and misrepresented by religious enemies; but he was as indifferent to all these charges as the limestone rocks of Elm Crag (Franklin College and Its Influences, by James E. Scobey, p. 219).

One of the fond remembrances Chisholm had of Franklin College was, while a student at Old Lasea, he returned to Franklin College one summer and became a part of a school trip to Huntsville, Alabama, with several professors and young men who were talented in singing. It was customary for college students to take trips with different professors to study or perform, as the case may be. The story of the young men from Franklin College performing in Huntsville, Alabama, is related below:

> When we reached Huntsville, Ala., we pitched our tent hard by the city, and announced a free concert in the courthouse that night (Friday). We had a fair audience, and the young men did full justice to the occasion. In the meantime the professors, who were all young men, began to be introduced to the young ladies of the city; and the boys followed their example, till the city was all aglow with promenades, flowers, and bouquets. The boys seemed to be on stilts, and at night the courthouse was jammed, while flowers showered like meteors upon the musicians. When the time came (to leave Huntsville), nearly every student and professor had a sweetheart that he must tell good-by. Finally he got them 'rounded up,' and we all had to double-quick to make the barbecue (<u>Franklin College and Its Influences</u>, by James E. Scobey, pp. 218-219).

The Chisholm family was neighbors not only to Professor James E. Scobey, but also to Tolbert and Charlotte Fanning. Chisholm said:

> I lived a near neighbor to Mr. Fanning and worshiped in the same congregation with him to the close of his eventful life. In speaking of Tolbert Fanning's death, Chisholm said, 'Mr. Fanning's death was premature, and resulted from his strong will. He died from internal hemorrhage from the following cause: One of Fanning's prize bulls had lunged at him, and came near killing him upon the spot; but he was carried to the house, and doctors were called in.'

Chisholm said he was with Fanning when he died.

> I was with him night and day till he died. On that Sunday morning it was evident to him that the end was

rapidly approaching, and he requested the brethren to hold services in his room. Though it was clear to all present that, he was rapidly sinking, he directed the entire service. A few minutes later two of his neighbor gentlemen called in. He called each by name and asked them to be seated. In less than five minutes he breathed his last, as if dropping off into a restful sleep.

When Dr. Chisholm died on December 3, 1913, after taking ill of pneumonia, a memorial service was held in Nashville with James E. Scobey and T. B. Larimore each speaking his thoughts in harmony with the occasion. The body was transported back to Tuscumbia, Alabama for burial. James E. Scobey, Chisholm's dear friend and neighbor, accompanied the body to Tuscumbia and spoke at the burial in Tuscumbia's Oakwood Cemetery. His message is recorded in the December 18, 1913 issue of the *Gospel Advocate*. He said in part:

> My dear friends, we have come to this place to bury the body of Dr. L. C. Chisholm, our friend and brother, not to praise him. He desired his body to rest in this spot on his native heath, at the place where he first saw the light of day over ninety-one years ago. I suppose there is not a man or woman present who played with him in his childhood days. Perhaps some are present who may have known him in his mature manhood. It has been my fortune to know him well in the latter years of his life. For forty-five years past I have observed his walk and conversation as he moved among men.
>
> I have said that we have come to bury him, not to praise him. Still, the time and circumstances seem to demand that I say something in eulogy of the splendid reputation he has made for a devoted, consecrated, Christian man: but the eulogy shall neither be fulsome nor extravagant—a simple recital of bare facts as I see them.
>
> The whole tenor of his life seems to have been attuned to the music of God's love, which constrained

him at all times, to endeavor to walk in the paths of peace and righteousness.

In 1850,* sixty-three years ago, he enlisted as a solider of the cross and began to fight the good fight of faith under the blood-stained banner of the Prince of Peace. The weapons of his warfare were not carnal, but mighty, because he became strong in the Lord and the power of his might. He put on the whole of the Christian armor, and has wielded the sword of the Spirit—the word of God—often to the discomfiture of those who assailed what he conceived to be the truth, both by word and pen. He was a writer of no mean ability. He contributed much to the periodicals published by his brethren. He was a man of strong convictions, and he possessed the courage and the ability necessary to sustain them, if they could be sustained.

He obeyed the gospel and became a Christian under the preaching of that prince of bible teachers and strong defenders of its precepts, Tolbert Fanning, at Russellville, Ala., in 1850.* He determined then and there, by the grace of God, to seek for and obtain the blessing and privileges of the kingdom of Christ on earth, and by a faithful continuance in well doing to seek for glory, honor, and eternal life; and from that day to the close of his earthly career he steadfastly pursued the way that leads to life. He had great faith in God's goodness and mercy and a confiding reliance in his promises. He had his trials, tribulations, disappointments, and sorrow; but his trusting confidence and hope in God was simply beautiful. In one of the misfortunes which came to him, I wrote him a letter of sympathy. He answered by writing me one; and I want to read you an extract from that letter. He says; 'The love of the world is enmity with Christ, and the glory of man is bubble on the ocean of time; but the word of the Lord endureth forever. I, therefore, trust in his promises revealed in the gospel of Christ. By these thoughts, God gives me strength to bear the afflictions of life as a true soldier of the cross. My life is an open book, and whatever the world may think of it shall not turn my mind from trusting in God and his promises in the gospel of Christ.' His life should be, and is, a benediction to his family and friends.

Of course, he was not a man without faults; but I never heard his general conduct condemned, his integrity impeached, nor his honesty questioned. He leaves to his children and friends the heritage of a good name. Let them sorrow for him, but not without hope that they may meet him again in the 'sweet by and by.'

'I heard a voice from heaven saying unto me, Write, Blessed are the dead which die in the Lord from henceforth Yea, saith the Spirit, that they may rest from their labors, and their works do follow them.'

Though Chisholm lived the last half of his life in Nashville, his death was reported with great sadness in Tuscumbia, Alabama, where many years before he had erected a gravestone for himself and his two wives who had preceded him in death. *The Alabamian-Dispatch* newspaper reported the death on Thursday, December 4, 1913, and carried a lengthy obituary on December 11, 1913. The obituary began with the heading, "Death of Dr. Lewis C. Chisholm," and as a subheading the words, "A Good Man Has Passed O'er The River into the Great and Mysterious Beyond." In part, the obituary stated:

> Dr. Lewis C. Chisholm, for many years a popular resident of Tuscumbia, but late of Nashville, died at the home of his son-in-law, Mr. J. D. Pope, of that city last Friday, after a few days' illness of pneumonia. Dr. Chisholm was born in this city May 20th, 1822, and practiced dentistry here 50 years ago; He was an active man with a strong, clear mind up to his last illness and gave promise of living past the century mark.
>
> He was laid to rest in this city between his two wives, having years ago made all arrangements for his burial.
>
> He had erected his own monument, with his name and date of birth, many years ago, in fact so long ago

that the marble had become dark with age. He had arrangements made with the undertaker to chisel the date of his death, which will be done by undertaker Challen of this city. He was a devoted member of the Christian Church and was converted at a meeting held in Russellville 60 years ago. His pastor, Dr. Scoby (sic) who had been a neighbor and intimated friend of Dr. Chisholm and family for many years accompanied the remains with Mr. and Mrs. Pope, and his brother, Dr. Edmund Chisholm, of St. Louis. Dr. Scoby (sic) was assisted in the service by Rev. Colemon of Sheffield. Dr. Scoby (sic) who had been a neighbor and intimate friend for many years delivered a most beautiful and touching eulogy. A selected choir delivered solemn and sacred music, while the remains of the grand old man was laid to rest beneath the great oaks and among the hills of old North Alabama, where he was wont to play in childhood nearly a century ago.

Dr. L. C. Chisholm was laid to rest in the home of his youth. He was buried where he was born, where his parents obeyed the gospel, where he ran and played as a child, and conducted a successful dental practice as an adult. Here he brought his young wife, and it was here that his children were born. He was buried a short distance from Locust Hill, the site of his beautiful home that was ransacked during the Civil War and where his first wife, Jane, died shortly after the atrocities of the Union Army at their home.

Dr. Chisholm is not remembered for his preaching but for his life of faithfulness to Christ. The Church and every community would be much better off today if there were more men like Dr. Lewis Clark Chisholm.

*Professor James E. Scobey records the wrong date of Chisholm's conversion. It was in early 1842, not in 1850.

Chapter 13

The Rise and Demise of Jesse B. Ferguson

In 1932, when H. Leo Boles published his book, <u>Biographical Sketches of Gospel Preachers</u>, he included a sketch on Jesse B. Ferguson. In his introductory statement about Ferguson, Boles made a statement that has been quoted over the years, describing Ferguson as one of most talented and brilliant gospel preachers who ever lived. Boles wrote:

> Like a meteor which flashes across the horizon, making a trail of glorious light behind it, and then suddenly disappearing and leaving nothing but darkness in its wake, so Jesse B. Ferguson came above the horizon and shone as a great pulpit orator in the church of Christ at Nashville, Tenn., and then as suddenly disappeared and dropped into obscurity. Perhaps no preacher of the gospel ever stood so high in the estimation of the people and received the plaudits of the populace and then dropped so low as did this man.

No gospel preacher who ever lived came from more humble beginnings and achieved so much adulation only to fall from popularity to obscurity. The man who once brought a sense of importance to people on the streets of Nashville, Tennessee, by simply recognizing and speaking to them, became a man hardly spoken to and recognized on the very same streets not many years later. The old saying, "The bigger the man, the harder the fall" certainly applied to Ferguson. He was the most popular man in Nashville in the early 1850s, but in a short time he fell from the grace of those who elevated him to such a position.

Over the years, Ferguson has been described as a gifted writer, forceful orator, great pulpit orator, popular orator, esteemed orator, greatest pulpit orator that ever visited Nashville, a very fascinating and eloquent speaker, and one who enjoyed greater prominence and popularity than any denominational preacher. It was said that his preaching was powerful, and when Ferguson preached in Nashville, the church of Christ enjoyed a greater prominence and popularity than any of the denominational churches, and that the citizens of Nashville considered it an honor to be recognized by him when they met him on the streets.

But there were other adjectives and descriptions used to describe Ferguson that were not as flattering. It has been written that he was spoiled and conceited. He had much egotism, and enjoyed the fame. He loved popularity. He was erratic, and a politician. He veered the way the popular winds seemed to blow, and was ambitious. David Lipscomb said of Ferguson that he "had not humility of soul and strength o character to stand flattery and adulation heaped upon him."

With such great contradictions in character, Jesse B. Ferguson was setting himself up for a great fall. When Alexander Campbell reviewed Ferguson's writings on spiritualism, he immediately realized that Ferguson was a "loose cannon" and would destroy the church in Nashville if not stopped. For this reason, Campbell wrote many articles in the *Millennial Harbinger* exposing Ferguson as a false teacher and came to Nashville for the purpose of debating him. Ferguson refused, claiming he had a spirit communication from the deceased Dr. William E. Channing, advising Ferguson to have nothing to do with Campbell. Ferguson failed to show up at the meetings. This caused a decline in Ferguson's popularity.

Early Life of Ferguson

Jesse Babcock Ferguson was born January 19, 1819, in Philadelphia, Pennsylvania. When he was very young, the family moved to Virginia. At the age of eleven, Jesse was a student at Fair View Academy and performed well in his studies. His older brothers had been educated at William and Mary College, in Williamsburg, Virginia. But Jesse's father had some financial reverses that resulted in not being able to send Jesse to college. Instead, at the age of thirteen, Jesse was apprenticed by his father to a printer to learn the printing trade. Soon after the beginning of his apprenticeship, the printer who was training him failed in business and released Jesse from his apprenticeship. His father, determined to give his son a trade, soon found another printer to take Jesse in Baltimore, Maryland. After a short time, Jesse became ill. Losing his health, he returned home. About this time, one of Jesse's brothers became the editor of a newspaper and gave Jesse a job. Jesse was able to work and continue his education, studying Latin and Greek.

When he was twenty-one, Jesse moved to the frontier of Ohio and opened a school. While there, he married and soon thereafter moved to Kentucky. In 1838, Jesse began to preach. His talent as a speaker was immediately noted, and success seemed to follow him as he converted many to Christ and established a number of churches. Soon he became known as a sophisticated preacher, and compliments and praises of men were heaped on him. Jesse seemed to find his place in life, but the compliments and praises would soon give rise to egotism and eventually his loss to the cause of Christ and his own spirituality.

As Ferguson's popularity as a preacher increased, so did the invitations to speak at other churches. Ferguson found himself holding a number of protracted meetings. His fame spread throughout Kentucky, and soon he was receiving invitations to speak at churches from other states. By 1842, his popularity had reached Nashville, Tennessee. At this time, no one could have predicted the popularity Ferguson would have in Nashville, as he became the "darling" of the town. In 1848, writing in the *Christian Magazine*, Ferguson boasted that he had preaching calls from Memphis, New York City, and the state of Ohio.

Ferguson's Work in Nashville, Tennessee

The church of Christ in Nashville had its beginning in 1826 when Phillip Slater Fall, a twenty-seven year old Baptist preacher, came to Nashville from Louisville, Kentucky. At first, Fall refused an invitation to preach for the Baptist church, focusing his attention on his position as a faculty member of the Nashville Female Institute. Influenced by the writings of Alexander Campbell, Fall began a prayerful study of the New Testament, and soon became convinced that the Bible was the all-sufficient guide in matters of religion. This led him to put away his Baptist Creed. When asked again to preach for the Baptist Church, Fall said he would accept their invitation if the church would accept his newly found truth in matters of religion. Fall was assured that many in Nashville shared his views, and Fall preached in Nashville until 1831. When Fall returned to Kentucky in 1831, the Nashville church looked to a young man from Lauderdale County, Alabama, who had come to Nashville to attend the University of Nashville. Soon, this young man, Tolbert Fanning, was working with the church. Tolbert Fanning had been taught the truth under James E. Matthews and was one of four young people baptized at a gospel meeting held on Cypress Creek, near Florence, Alabama, in September 1826. The preacher in this meeting was B. F. Hall. Hall and Fanning would work together years later in the Nashville area.

The 1842 gospel meeting held at the Nashville church of Christ with Jesse B. Ferguson as the speaker was a huge success. Ferguson was urged to locate in Nashville and work with the church. He declined the offer but returned two years later in 1844 to hold another meeting. This meeting was also a success and the church again begged him to locate in Nashville. Again, Ferguson declined the offer. However, in 1846, Ferguson accepted the invitation to come to Nashville and work with the church.

Dr. W. H. Wharton had for the past few years been preaching for the Nashville church. He moved to Nashville from Tuscumbia, Alabama, where he started a church in 1832. Wharton learned the truth from Walter Scott's paper, *The Evangelist*. He left the Presbyterian Church and joined the Baptist Church, thinking that they were closer to the religion of the New Testament. Wharton soon realized that he could not continue believing in the necessity of baptism for the remission of sins and remain with the Baptists.

Dr. Wharton made his living as a medical doctor. As the church in Nashville grew, the demands on the preacher became greater. Wharton was ready for some relief in the pulpit, and Ferguson was believed to be the right man for the job.

About the time Ferguson came to Nashville, Tolbert Fanning was also looking for a change, wanting to spend less time with his paper, *Christian Review*, and more time promoting Franklin College, of which Fanning was founder and president. Fanning, like most members of the church, was enthralled with the young preacher Ferguson. In 1847, Fanning was looking for an editor for the paper and asked Ferguson to take the position. Ferguson accepted, and immediately changed the name to *Christian Magazine*. With a background in printing and publishing, Ferguson decided to make the paper more attractive and somewhat larger. Ferguson introduced the new paper by writing:

> We need a work suited to the times in size, spirit and matter. We have been often and earnestly solicited to commence such a work; but until recently, owing to the fact that we have so many publications, but meagerly sustained, we have hesitated and declined.

> But in our present enterprise this difficulty is removed; we enlarge and seek to improve an existing periodical, while we have thrown around us increased facilities for making a paper such as we desire. . . To our friends in the South and South-west, especially, we look for support. Theirs is a somewhat new and uncultivated field of labor (West, Search for the Ancient Order, vol. I, p. 262).

Ferguson introduced this new publication with B. F. Hall and Tolbert Fanning as editors. But this arrangement was brief. In 1850, John Eichbaum was chosen associate editor. He served in this position for about two years.

During the time Ferguson preached for the church in Nashville, the church had tremendous growth, outgrowing their house of worship. Plans were made to build a new building, one that would seat twelve hundred worshipers. The church sold its old building, and moved into the new building on Cherry Street. But shortly after the construction of this building, the church split over Ferguson's teaching on spiritualism. The vast majority of the members supported Ferguson and retained possession of the new place of worship.

In December 1855, the elders of the church notified Ferguson that he would no longer preach for the church. Ferguson refused to vacate the pulpit or his house. On the last Sunday in 1855, Ferguson read a letter signed by five men, asking him to stay on as the preacher. Interestingly, none of the five were members of the church. By this time, the members were tired of the problems surrounding Ferguson, and only one-third wanted him to stay. The division was bitter, and it appeared that the matter would have to be settled in the courts. However, Ferguson resigned, eliminating a lawsuit.

While this was going on, the matter of the ownership of the building was still in question, with the followers of Ferguson retaining the building. The smaller group sued the

Ferguson faction in Chancery Court for possession of the building and the smaller group finally gained possession in December 1856. It has been said that in the building built to seat twelve hundred worshippers, there were only fifteen to twenty-five persons left to fill the seats. In February, the elders of the church, (James H. Foster, J. D. March, and Frank McGavock) announced that the property matter had been cleared up. By this time, Ferguson had shown his true colors, left the church, and joined a denomination. On April 8, 1857, the building mysteriously caught on fire and burned to the ground. It was believed that some of Ferguson's followers set the fire that destroyed the building. The church was able to rent the old building they had sold, and in a few months were able to repurchase it. It was reported at this time that there were forty-two white people and fourteen colored who were snatched from Ferguson's influence. This was about ten percent of the former congregation before the destruction brought on by Jesse B. Ferguson.

Ferguson's Fall from Grace

Ferguson's fall from the good graces of the members of the church of Christ began in 1852 when he published an article in *Christian Magazine* titled, *Spirits in Prison*. In this article, Alexander Campbell said that Ferguson believed in a posthumous gospel, and Ferguson had come to believe the deceased would have another opportunity for salvation.

In Ferguson's article on *Spirits in Prison*, he took the verses, 1 Peter 3:18-19, to mean that Jesus offers a second chance at salvation to those who have departed this life. These verses say, "For Christ also suffered once for sins, the just for the unjust, that He might bring us to God, being put to death in the flesh but made alive by the Spirit, by whom also He went and preached to the spirits in prison."

This passage is universally recognized as a difficult passage. Ferguson's explanation was that Christ went to the realm of the dead, preached to the spirits of doomed men, and offered them a second chance at salvation. There are two great problems with this position. First, it violates several scriptures that point out that the fate of man is sealed at the time of death. Hebrews 9:27 says, "And as it is appointed for men to die once, but after this the judgment." 2 Peter 2:4-5 says, "For if God did not spare the angels who sinned, but cast them down to hell and delivered them into chains of darkness, to be reserved for judgment; and did not spare the ancient world, but saved Noah, one of eight people, a preacher of righteousness, bringing in the flood on the world of the ungodly." 2 Peter 2:9 says, "The Lord knows how to deliver the godly out of temptations and to reserve the unjust under punishment for the Day of Judgment."

Second, Ferguson misapplied the scripture to say that Christ preached to the spirits of men, and offered men a second chance at salvation. The passage says, he "preached to spirits" and not to the spirits of men. The Bible makes plain the subject of the spirits or souls of men, and such terminology is used in Hebrews 12:23, Revelation 6:9, and Revelation 20:4. A common interpretation of this passage is that Christ preached to the spirits of angels and not to the spirits of men. The Book of Jude and also 2 Peter 2, speaks of the angels who were disobedient. They are "reserved in everlasting chains under darkness unto the judgment of the great day" (Jude 6), and that "God spared not the angels that sinned, but cast them down to hell, and delivered them into chains of darkness, to be reserved unto judgment" (2 Peter 2:4). The explanation seems to be that, despite the suffering and death of Christ, He was made alive and proclaimed victory to those spirits who had not been willing to submit to God in Noah's day.

This article was the first glimpse into the heart of a man who was already trying to make contact with the dead and conducting séances to conjure up the dead. This within itself was a violation of the scriptures. Notice these examples:

Deuteronomy 18:10-11 There shall not be found among you anyone who makes his son or his daughter pass through the fire, or one who practices witchcraft, or a soothsayer, or one who interprets omens, or a sorcerer, or one who conjures spells, or a medium, or a spiritist, or one who calls up the dead.

Leviticus 19:31 Give no regard to mediums and familiar spirits; do not seek after them, to be defiled by them: I am the LORD your God.

Leviticus 20:6 And the person who turns to mediums and familiar spirits, to prostitute himself with them, I will set My face against that person and cut him off from his people.

Isaiah 8:19 And when they say to you, "Seek those who are mediums and wizards, who whisper and mutter," should not a people seek their God? Should they seek the dead on behalf of the living?

What seemed to many as a new explanation of a passage of scripture was immediately noticed and denounced by the famous gospel preacher, Alexander Campbell. From Bethany, Campbell attacked Ferguson through the pages of the *Millennial Harbinger*. Campbell's first attack on Ferguson was in the July 1852 edition of the *Millennial Harbinger*. Campbell, speaking of the article by Ferguson on the "Spirits in Prison," wrote:

> It is, therefore, presumed to be a defence (sic) from the imputations arising from his views of a posthumous mission to the dead, in order to translate them from a miserable prison to heaven. We should think indeed, that it must needs be a short mission and a universal conversion. For, who in a place of torment, or in any uncomfortable position in hades, would need much urging to accept an invitation to come out, and to ascend to leave?

Alexander Campbell realized that this teaching could destroy the church. He, therefore, wrote several articles in the *Millennial Harbinger* refuting Ferguson's position. He even came to Nashville to debate Ferguson, but Ferguson declined. As stated earlier, Ferguson claimed that the spirit of a dead man, Dr. William E. Channing, advised him to have nothing to do with Campbell. After this, Ferguson's influence declined and so did the church in Nashville. Campbell was right in his assessment that Ferguson's teaching would destroy the church.

Book on Spiritualism

In 1854, Ferguson published a book titled, <u>Spirit Communication: A Record of Communications from the Spirit Spheres</u>. In this book, Ferguson documents thirty-one communications through séances in which he talked with the spirits of the dead. This book is 287 pages long. This writer was fortunate to secure a copy of it. By looking at some of Ferguson's quotes found in this book, one can readily see that he had left the faith and was consumed with a preoccupation with spirit communication.

On spirit communication, Ferguson wrote:

> Men are too apt to approach Spirits as though they were ghosts of a false imagination. When convinced of this mistake, their next approach is as if they were gods. In neither case are they prepared for just or rational conclusions. Neither the inflation of pride, nor the indifference of sensualism (sic), can receive any truth in its symmetrical proportions. What a supercilious vanity, or a frenzied fanaticism, or a silly contempt would call a contradiction, a more teachable and candid mind would regard as a striking evidence of individuality preserved.

On spiritualism and the Bible, Ferguson wrote:

> This objection only reveals the lack of faith in the claims made for the Bible, on the part of those who use

it. No truth in the Bible can be destroyed. Many false conceptions of its teachings will be exposed by Spiritualism, as many have been exposed by every advance of the human mind. But truth is Eternal and will out-last all blind reverence for what is superstitiously regarded as sacred and divine. The Bible is a collection of Spiritual Communications, as unequal, and as characteristically progressive as the Spiritual illuminations of our times. A false claim for them endangers our reverence for the Book more than any developments of modern Spiritualism. If He who consulted the Spirits of Moses and Elias could say, 'Verily I say unto you of all born of woman there has not one arisen equal to John the Baptist, but the least in the kingdom of Heaven shall be greater than he,' we may believe him, rather than those who make false claims of infallibility for the imprecations of David or the cruel laws of Moses. The example of Jesus and John in consulting Spirits is of more value upon this subject, upon the acknowledged principles of our opportunity.

Ferguson wrote concerning Christianity:

> Spiritualism has not the tendency to subvert true Christianity. It is for the enlightenment and universal good of all men that these great and sublime theories are addressed to their reason. Truth alone will subvert error, and show us what true Christianity is ; nor will it rob her of any of those virtues which should adorn her; nor will it disarm her of all those great and moral precepts which are universally taught, but, alas not practiced. True, this is an age of enlightenment.

On believing in God and rejecting spiritualism, Ferguson wrote:

> Do you believe in God!—And yet believe not in the communion of His holy Spirits! It cannot be. Reject not what alone can ennoble and hallow your desires. True, much that professes to come from spirits, ought not to

be countenanced. But is this our fault or yours? Rest assured you must judge; but how can you judge when you are not true to the purest and deepest thirst of your own souls? Remember spirits have to use imperfect mediums. Remember your own imperfections; of which you need no better evidence, than your unnatural and sinful prejudices against, what you know, ought to make for your highest good. Be true to yourselves, and you will know how to discriminate. Know that nothing but the pure can come from God, and his holy messengers. We come from him to invite you to brighter thoughts, hopes and visions, than have ever blessed the walks or ways of the most enlightened mortals. And now may the Spirit of God rest upon this American People, and bind them as one congenial band of brothers.

On the inspiration and authority of the Bible, Ferguson wrote:

The certainty of communion with high-born Spirits of another sphere, and through them with the Great Spirit of all Wisdom and Love, from whom in our own souls, according to the degree of their purity and freedom, we receive all truth and power, very naturally leads to the question: What think you of the Bible? We have already stated, what we believe no honest investigation will invalidate, that the Bible is a collection of Spiritual Communications, of unequal character, varying in the degree of their light and help, according to the capacity of the individuals through whom they were made, and the necessities of the age that received them. It must be manifest to every observing mind, that there is a blind and idolatrous reverence for the Bible, derogatory alike to the native powers of human Reason and Intuition, and to the writers of that Book. Men are taught to reverence the Book more than the indisputable and inspiring truths it records.

They claim the Book as an infallible revelation from God, when it makes no such claim for itself, and they quote its passages, which speak of the Scriptures as inspired, and of the terrible consequences of adding to, or taking from its revelations, and apply such quotations to the present collection of Books, forgetting that such declarations were made before the present collection was made, and that they had special reference to some distinct revelation, made for a specified object, which object has long since been secured.

Ferguson went on to say, "All men are mediums; but mediumship has its degrees. The high degrees here presented, with all their attendant difficulties detailed, are intended only to inspire to still higher, as men prepare themselves for Spiritual guests."

He also spoke of hell as fiction. He wrote: "The terrors of a Hell are a dark and idle fiction of equally dark and perverted intellects. Give all heed to the great and glorious illustrations of God's goodness, and spiritual illumination will dispel this horrible libel upon the nature of man and the purposes of God."

Ferguson's downfall was almost complete. It is obvious from these statements and others that, before leaving the pulpit in the Nashville Church of Christ, J. B. Ferguson had left the faith and carried many away with him.

Travels with the Davenports

After Ferguson's fall from the faith, he traveled with the Davenport Brothers (William and Ira), who were magicians. The brothers reportedly were able to do the amazing things they did because of spiritualism and supernatural events. Ferguson traveled with them extensively, even to England, serving as the "opening act." He would lecture on spiritualism before the Davenports came on stage and worked their tricks. Ferguson was seemingly sincere in what he said, and he assured the audience that the brothers worked by the power of the spirits, rather than by trickery.

The Davenports most famous trick was the box illusion, where the brothers were tied inside a box that contained musical instruments. The box was closed, and the instruments would sound. Upon opening the box, the brothers were tied in the positions they were in when the trick began. The effect was that supernatural forces had caused the trick to work.

Magicians John Henry Anderson and Jan Eugene Robert-Houdin worked to expose the Davenports as "phonies" by performing duplicate effects. On one occasion, two magicians tied the Davenports into their box with a knot that could not be easily removed, and the trick was exposed. P. T. Barnum included an expose of the Davenports in his 1865 book, <u>The Humbugs of the World</u>. The famous escape artist, Harry Houdini, was skeptical of spiritualism and never made such claims to his audiences. Houdini always made it clear to his audiences that his feats were the result of skill, not supernatural occurrences.

Later Life

After traveling with the Davenports, Ferguson returned to Nashville. Now, a virtual unknown, he was no longer acknowledged on the streets of Nashville as the great man he once was. Many who had known him in the past refused to speak to him.

Ferguson had made some good financial investments and a good deal of money in real estate. If the size of a grave stone is an indication of one's wealth (and often it is), Ferguson was a very wealthy man. His grave marker at Mt. Olivet Cemetery in Nashville is probably the largest in the city and maybe in the state of Tennessee. It is a large column with an angel gracing the top. The stone is probably twenty to twenty-five feet in height. Several members of his family are buried in the vicinity of the great monument. The inscription on the stone simply says:

Jesse B. Ferguson, D.D.
Born Jan. 19, 1819;
Died Sept. 3, 1870.

Positive and Negative Affects of Ferguson's Fall

As one ponders the positive and negative affects of Jesse Ferguson, the positives may be a short list. Negatively, Jesse Ferguson destroyed one of the largest churches of Christ in the country with his teaching on spiritualism. The church of Christ became a group looked down on by the vast majority of people in Nashville. The church lost its influence, lost its building, lost its credibility, and lost its way, becoming almost completely annihilated during a time of great spiritual growth in a community that desperately needed it.

Can there be positives to the Ferguson fiasco? One of the greatest lessons learned was not to put one's faith in a man. Preacheritis (following popular preachers) is dangerous. Paul mentioned this problem in the church at Corinth in 1 Corinthians 1, when he warned of following various men. The Christians in Nashville learned this lesson.

Perhaps the greatest positive is that after Ferguson had almost destroyed the faith of the young man, David Lipscomb. Lipscomb rebounded spiritually and began to study the Bible more deeply and he became the most popular member of the church in Nashville, not only as a preacher, but also as an educator, by establishing Nashville Bible School. The conservative views of David Lipscomb saved the churches in Tennessee from the division over the missionary society and musical instruments in worship.

Death of Jesse B. Ferguson

On September 4, 1870, the notice of Ferguson's death appeared in the Nashville Union and American, a daily paper published in Nashville. The notice stated:

DEATH OF REV. J. B. FERGUSON

We are pained to chronicle this morning the death of our eminent fellow citizen, Rev. J. B. Ferguson, who died at his residence yesterday morning, three miles from the city, after a lingering disease. Some years ago, when Mr. Ferguson was pastor of the Christian Church, he enjoyed a reputation for pulpit oratory second to no man in the South. He commenced life as a printer's boy, and was emphatically a self-made man, having by studious attention, while employed at the printing business, fitted himself for the ministry. He was a man of popular manners, warm and open-hearted in his nature, and generally esteemed by a large circle of friends.

David Lipscomb, so disturbed by the fiasco years before, almost lost his faith over Ferguson's fall. However, he rebounded spiritually by determining to make a deeper study of the scriptures, and became the most important figure in churches of Christ in post-war Nashville. He wrote of Ferguson's death in the September 22, 1870 issue of *Gospel Advocate*:

It may be a matter of sad interest to our readers to know the fate of this once honored but erratic man. He was the most popular preacher in the Southern country at one time. He was almost worshiped by his admirers in this city, where he ministered as preacher of the church of Christ. He had not that humility of soul and strength of character to stand flattery and adulation heaped upon him. He apostatized from the faith and adopted latitudinarian views in his faith and with reference to morality. He attempted to build up a congregation of adherents on his loose views. He failed, turned politician, veered to different points of the compass as the popular winds seemed to blow. He lost respect of all parties here. Once no citizen of Nashville but felt it an honor to be recognized by him. In later years he was scarcely recognized by his former acquaintances even of the world when met on the streets. The contrast was too painful to be borne by one so ambitious of popular applause as he. So, although his family resided in the vicinity, of late years he was seldom upon the streets of Nashville. . . He died on Saturday, September 3, 1870. On Lord's day he was buried at Mount Olivet Cemetery. The funeral services were performed by Dr. Baird, of the Cumberland Presbyterian Church.

If Jesse B. Ferguson lived today and chose to do so, he could be a multi-millionaire preacher of the prime time brand. There is probably no preacher today with the ability to move people as Ferguson could.

There are lessons to be learned from Jesse Ferguson. The mistakes Ferguson made should not be repeated, and his teachings are not to be followed.

Jesse B. Ferguson

Chapter 14

The Gospel Preacher Condemned to Death by Hanging

Mansel Matthews

Mansel Matthews was one of the great gospel preachers of the nineteenth century. He was born December 29, 1806, in Kentucky, and then moved to Tennessee, where his youth was spent. In the 1820's, Mansel moved to Lauderdale County, Alabama, where he came under the influence of several members of the church of Christ. Matthews said, "I confessed my Savior and was buried with him in baptism by brother John Mulkey in Spring Creek, Franklin County (now Colbert County), Alabama, in 1823" and "commenced publicly proclaiming His cause in 1825." Mansel Matthews studied dentistry and medicine, but his first love seemed to be preaching. His early labors brought him in close association with Barton Stone, Walter Scott, John T. Johnston, "Raccoon" John Smith, John Mulkey, John Newton Mulkey, Ephraim D. Moore, and Thacker Griffin. Immediately after his conversion, Mansel Matthews began to preach, and following the example set by Alexander Campbell (whether consciously following Campbell we do not know), he never accepted pay for his preaching. He had other plans. He went to Kentucky, studied medicine, and became a recognized physician.

All his life, he engaged in both medicine and preaching. Dr. Matthews preached for the Waterloo church of Christ in

Lauderdale County, Alabama when at home, but was often away with Benjamin Lynn D'Spain in protracted meetings. Much of their meeting work was done in Western Tennessee where, perhaps, they first came in contact with David Crockett, a former member of the U. S. House of Representatives and one of the most prominent and popular people in America. Crockett was "hankering" to go to Texas and fight in the Texas War of Independence.

Texas was the new "Promised Land" of the 1830s, just as Alabama had been after the turn of the century. Many Alabamians were interested in Texas. Perhaps the land along the Tennessee River at Waterloo had lost its productivity by the annual flooding of the river, or perhaps repeated crops had just worn out the land. The idea of vast expanses of land that could be had at a cheap price was enticing to many members of the church of Christ in Waterloo. Crockett was persuaded to serve as guide for the members of the church of Christ in Waterloo, Alabama, and many, if not most of them, decided to go to Texas. The church at that time is estimated to be about 300 members. This estimate is based on the order of 300 songbooks by the church at Waterloo in 1832, from Barton W. Stone (*Christian Messenger*, p. 380, 1832). This was probably one of the largest churches of Christ in the world at that time.

In the fall of 1835, this group from Waterloo left Alabama for Texas. This church has been referred to in history books as the "church on foot, on wheels and on horseback." The group from Waterloo, with women, children, and animals, moved too slowly for David Crockett. No doubt, the group also refused to travel on the "first day of the week" because it was a day of worship and rest. Perhaps for these reasons, and Crockett's desire to get to Texas as fast as he could, Crockett left the church members in Memphis and hurried to Texas, only to be killed at the Alamo, in March of 1836.

Dr. Mansel Matthews and Benjamin Lynn D'Spain led the church from Memphis, Tennessee (where Crockett left them), to Texas. The church arrived in Red River County on January 17, 1836, and settled in Clarksville, and then near Nacogdoches where the first church of Christ in Texas came into existence. After settling his family and winning the March 17 election as representative from Red River County to the First Texas Congress, Dr. Mansel Matthews joined the Texas army and served as a surgeon until July 1836. He was at the battle of San Jacinto and attended the wounded General Sam Houston when Houston's soldiers brought General Antonio López de Santa Anna to Houston as a captive. One of Benjamin Lynn D'Spain's brothers, Randolph D'Spain, joined the Texas army and was killed in the massacre at the Battle of Goliad when General Santa Anna ordered the execution of 400 captives.

For almost thirty years, Dr. Matthews served as a preacher in Texas. However, the Civil War brought new problems for Dr. Matthews. Mansel Matthews opposed secession, and a union sympathizer in a Confederate State made Dr. Matthews a very unpopular man. In 1864, while traveling in a caravan, Dr. Matthews was arrested on charges of treason and arraigned before the "high vigilance committee" in Gainesville, Texas. This committee was notorious and had already hanged a great number of men for treason. This committee, formed to break up a "Unionist Peace Party Plot" aimed at revolt against the Confederate government in Texas, was discovered in September 1862. Prompt action by local authorities broke up the organization in October 1862. Following a declaration of martial law in Cooke County, a "Citizen's Court," or jury, of twelve men composed of army officers and civilians was formed at Gainesville. It found thirty-nine of the participants guilty and sentenced them to be hanged for conspiracy and insurrection. Three other prisoners, who were members of military units, were permitted trial by court martial as they requested and were subsequently hanged by its order.

The committee, knowing that Dr. Mansel Matthews was a "union sympathizer," held court and found Dr. Matthews guilty of treason and sentenced him to die by "hanging from the neck until dead." E. M. Daggett from Fort Worth heard about this matter and traveled to Gainesville to plead for Matthews' life. He told the court that "Matthews mind may be with the North, but his heart is with the South." Evidently persuaded, the court commuted the death sentence to three days in jail, but instructions were given that Matthews was not to be told of the court's decision. This obviously was done for one purpose only, that Matthews might suffer for three more days, knowing in his heart that he would be hanged. Matthews had received the death sentence and was certain that it would be carried out. Daggett, who thought the portion of the new verdict (the part about not telling Matthews that his life would be spared) was cruel, sought a way to let Matthews know his life had been spared. Daggatt asked to see Matthews and he was given permission to do so in the presence of a guard, but was instructed not tell Matthews that his life had been spared. When brought to Matthews' cell, Daggett began a lengthy discussion about the Bible, which soon caused the guard to become inattentive. Daggett then asked Matthews to quote his favorite Bible verse, and Matthews asked Daggett to do the same. Daggett replied, "Fret not thy gizzard and zizzle not thy whirligig; thy soul art saved." Matthews immediately realized that his sentence had been commuted, but was afraid to show any emotion so that the guard might notice him. He just looked at the floor and trembled.

Dr. Mansel Matthews survived the ordeal and lived on until 1891. In 1888, three years prior to his death, Dr. Matthews wrote a letter to David Lipscomb. In this letter, printed in the August 22, 1888 issue of the *Gospel Advocate*, he mentioned his early labors and how things had changed over the sixty-five years of his preaching. Speaking of the old pioneer preachers, Matthews wrote: "We went and labored without the hope of earthly reward. Our lives were freely spent expecting our reward beyond the cold river." He spoke of the difficulties in the old days when pioneer preachers wore copperas or jeans, tread down grass and swam water courses for the love of truth. He lamented that these old pioneer preachers now had to "stand aside as the young and stylish preachers with hair parted in the middle, sporting a massive chain, charm and diamond ring, were now the ones fit to advocate the cause of Christ."

Also in this letter, the eighty-one year old Matthews said to David Lipscomb, "Your position Bro. L. is right. May the Lord bless and lengthen your days to battle for His truth." Matthews also spoke against a current departure from the faith, which he referred to as "sanctified common sense calculated to destroy the labors of the glorious cause of Christ." Perhaps this is a reference to the current turmoil in the church over the use of a musical instrument in worship. This was a hot issue at that time.

Matthews' first wife died at Thornton, Texas in 1870 and in 1872, he married Margaret Spencer, with whom he had four children. During the last twenty years of his life, he lived in Wise County where he bought and sold land, preached, practiced medicine, and operated a drugstore in Paradise, Texas, with his son. He lived in Paradise for ten years and died there on April 13, 1891. Through his grandfather, Walter Matthews, Mansel was a descendant of Oliver Cromwell. His cousins, Joseph W. and James E. Matthews (brothers), were governor and auditor of Mississippi, respectively. James E. Matthews was a gospel preacher in Lauderdale County, Alabama, and preached in the Bartons community, about ten miles east of Waterloo, Alabama, where Mansel practiced medicine and preached

Bad things can happen to good people. This is evident from the scriptures as we look at the lives of the apostles. It is also evident from the history of the protestant reformation when many were persecuted for their belief in God. Dr. Matthews' story is just another in a long list of stories of good people who suffered wrong as they went about trying to do good.

Notice the words of the apostle Peter: "For to this you were called, because Christ also suffered for us, leaving us an example, that you should follow His steps: Who committed no sin, nor was deceit found in His mouth" (1 Peter 2:21-22).

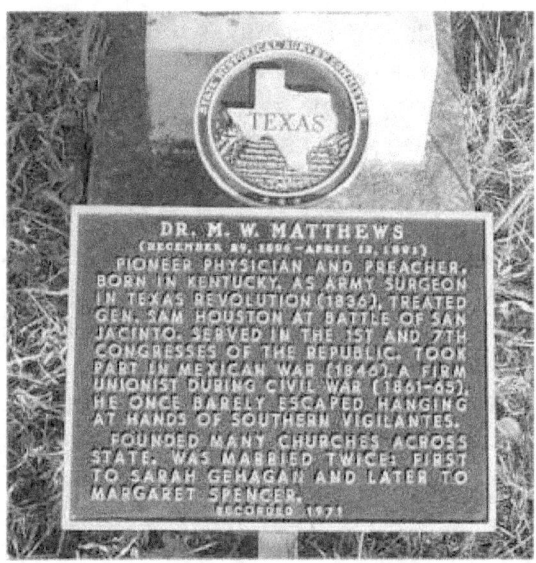

Grave of Dr. Mansel Matthews

Chapter 15

Saved By Uncle Sandy

John Dickie Wade was a member of the church of Christ when it was still relatively new to the regions of North Alabama and Southern Tennessee. He was born in Halifax County, Virginia, in 1814, and his great-grandson, Wade Pruitt, wrote in his book, "Bugger Saga," that Alexander Campbell baptized his grandfather. (This is unlikely, however. Another record shows that W. H. Wharton baptized him.) John Dickie was well educated, having been graduated from the Mechanical and Agricultural College, in Richmond. As an engineer, he was adept at building bridges and mills, or any project requiring his engineering skills. One of the bridges he built still spans the Tennessee River today.

John Dickie Wade was also a successful farmer. He had a plantation on the state line of Tennessee and Alabama. He named his plantation "Egypt," because his plantation was so successful in growing corn that people would come to him in "dry" years to buy. During the Civil War, cotton prices jumped to $1.40 per pound. In 1865, Wade sold $12,000.00 worth of cotton in Nashville, and he brought the money back home in gold coin, cleverly concealed in a hollowed out ox yoke. Wade hid his money in three places: some under the stairs of his home, some in the graves of his father and mother-in-law, and the rest was in the hollowed out ox yoke hanging in the barn in plain view.

News of such a large transaction was hard to keep secret, and on the night of April 9, 1865, thieves kicked in the front door of his plantation and demanded his money. They resorted to hanging John Dickie in front of his house. As they pulled him up and strangled him close to death, they would then let him down and ask where the money was hidden. This happened several times. This is when the hero of this story enters the picture.

Uncle Sandy was a former slave of John Dickie Wade. When he heard the commotion, he took quick action. The oldest son of John Dickie Wade, who had died in January of the same year in a Confederate prison camp, had owned a bugle. Uncle Sandy sent John Dickie's small son, John, to retrieve the bugle, while he rounded up as many relatives and former slaves as he could find in a few minutes. Under Uncle Sandy's instructions, this civilian army proceeded toward the house. Uncle Sandy told "Little Johnny" to blow the horn while Uncle Sandy yelled "Charge, charge them men, give not quarter." At this point, the rescuers delivered their most blood curdling Rebel yells while others rolled rocks down the hill toward the house. The women folks gathered on the porch and yelled, "The Rebels are coming, the Rebels are coming!" The thieves, thrown into confusion, fled, convinced that a more superior force was on its way. This was the first time the Wade's were saved by Uncle Sandy.

On another occasion, Uncle Sandy and his crew returned to the plantation home to find a company of Union soldiers on a foraging raid. Uncle Sandy had a surprise for them. He had recently "sacked" a large hornet's nest that he attached to a sapling tree and shot into the soldiers midst. This Civil War "A-Bomb" was extremely effective in dispersing the foragers.

One story about John Dickie Wade's "golden yoke" tells of a man called "Big John Hays" who carried off the yoke, without knowing the gold was in it. John Dickie let time take its course, and after the war was over, went to Hays and told him that the yoke had been one of the yokes used with a team of oxen that pulled his family's wagon from Halifax County, Virginia. He told Hays he was interested in buying the ox yoke. A price was finally agreed on, and Hays sold John Dickie's gold-filled yoke back to him for fifty cents.

Because of Wade's wealth and influence, and because of his dedication to the Lord's church, he helped further the cause of the restoration of the New Testament church in Northern Alabama and Southern Tennessee. This was especially true during the Civil War when the church all but disappeared in this area. When John Dickie Wade died in 1885, the great gospel preacher and Wade's personal friend, T. B. Larimore, wrote the *Gospel Advocate* to report the death of this man who influenced the spreading of the gospel during his lifetime. Larimore wrote:

> On the evening of November 14, 1885, our dear brother, John D. Wade, of Lawrence County, Tenn., was caught in machinery in his mill and terribly mangled. One arm was amputated. A few hours after the surgeon's knife had completed its work, our dear, faithful, suffering brother raised his hand, and, looking at it, said, 'I thank the Lord that I have one good hand left-I rejoice in the Lord- O, bless his name!' Such words were to be expected from such a man under such circumstances. These were nearly his last words, his sufferings terminating on the night of November 15, 1885. Brother Wade lived in the sunshine and shadows of earth seventy-three years and ten months, in the bright, blessed light of faith and hope and love in the church of Christ, more than half that time—forty years. Blessed brother, faithful friend, devoted disciple of the Lord -how we love you! How sad the thought-he is gone! We rejoice, even in the midst of sadness, to hear the Spirit say, 'Blessed are the dead which die in the Lord' (*Gospel Advocate*, May 26, 1886).

John Dickie Wade was buried in the Wade cemetery near Iron City, Tennessee, on his plantation, Egypt. Only a few feet away from his grave is another grave, a grave outlined with large hewn stones. The stone at the head simply says, "Uncle Sandy, ca 1825-1890." The man who had served John Dickie Wade was more than a servant; he had been a part of the Wade family. Under the influence of John Dickie Wade, Uncle Sandy was perhaps the first convert of color in Lauderdale County, Alabama, and the work of the church of Christ in the black community began with Uncle Sandy. Uncle Sandy was a brother in Christ to John Dickie Wade.

Grave of Uncle Sandy, Wade Cemetery, Iron City, Tennessee

Chapter 16

General Richard Montgomery Gano, CSA
General, Doctor, Gospel Preacher
1830-1913

His great-grandfather baptized George Washington. His great-grandson was the richest man in America when he died. His grandfather was a general in the War of 1812. His grandchildren were prominent citizens of Texas. His father is credited with baptizing more people in Kentucky than any other man. His son apprehended the murderer of William Lipscomb in a church service in Dallas, Texas. The story of the Gano family is rich in American history and even richer in restoration history. The focus of this story is on a gospel preacher and doctor—Richard Gano, who by time and chance became a general in the Confederate army. It was said of General Gano that he led his troops into battle, doctored their wounds, and preached to them on Sunday. After the war, Richard Gano became one of the richest men in Texas in a time when the South was economically destitute. The story of General Richard M. Gano is one that needs to be told. Preaching and military leadership were a part of his family, and in order to better understand General Gano's character, we need to look at those of his heritage who helped shape his life. We will begin with Richard's great grandfather.

Gen. R. M. Gano

The Gano Family

Richard M. Gano's great-grandfather was John Gano, personal chaplain of General George Washington. He was born at Hopewell, N.J., July 22, 1727, and was ordained to the ministry in 1754. He became a distinguished Baptist preacher and started the first Baptist church in New York City in 1762. He joined the army at the beginning of the Revolutionary War and remained in that service until Independence was established. Several accounts have been given of John Gano baptizing General George Washington. One of these accounts was written by the subject of this article, General Richard M. Gano, great-grandson of John Gano. Richard tells of visiting with his uncle, Captain Daniel Gano, who served under Washington, who told him the account of the baptism. He also mentions visiting with his eldest aunt, Mrs. Margaret Ewing, who told him of the baptism. Richard Gano wrote that General Washington said to his great-grandfather:

> Mr. Gano, I have been listening to you preach and examining the Scriptures. And I am satisfied that immersion is the scriptural mode of baptism. My family are Episcopalians and I have no desire to change my church, but I demand immersion at your hands.
> And in the presence of about 42 witnesses, John Gano led Gen. Washington down into the river and baptized him. It was near Valley Forge, in the Hudson river (Gano box, Disciples of Christ Historical Society, Nashville, Tennessee).

Richard M. Gano's story of the baptism of George Washington dispels the story that has been passed around for years that some in the Gano family said General Washington was baptized for the remission of sins. It seems from this account that Washington simply questioned the mode of baptism of the Episcopalians and demanded immersion. For this reason, the Baptists claim George Washington as one of their own, and a painting of George Washington being immersed by John Gano hangs in Gano Chapel, William Jewell College, in Liberty, Missouri.

John Gano's four sons were successful: one (Dr. Stephen Gano) being a physician and three of them were military officers. They were Captain Daniel Gano (Revolutionary War), Major General John Stiles Gano (War of 1812), and Brigadier General Richard Montgomery Gano (War of 1812). General Richard Montgomery Gano was the grandfather and namesake of the Richard Gano of this article. He was born in 1775, and died at the age of forty in 1815. His son, John Allen Gano, being only ten years old when his father died, was raised by an uncle, Captain William Hubble of the War of 1812.

Richard Gano's Father, John Allen Gano

Richard Gano's father was John Allen Gano. He was born at Georgetown, Kentucky, on July 14, 1805, and died on October 11, 1887. John Allen Gano's beautiful mansion near Georgetown still stands today, and it seems that John Allen Gano lived a life of affluence. John Allen became an attorney and planned to go to Texas to practice his profession in that state. However, while traveling to Texas on a steamer, he became dangerously ill and was put off at some point in the lower Ohio. During his sickness, he pledged to God that if he recovered he would preach. He returned home and married Mary Catherine Conn, the daughter of a neighbor and a member of one of the prominent families of Kentucky.

John Allen Gano had been a student of Barton Stone at Writtenhouse Academy at Georgetown and was familiar with Stone's teaching. In 1826, he attended a meeting held by Stone and T. M. Allen and converted to New Testament Christianity, repenting, confessing, and being baptized. His family was so upset by his decision to leave the Baptist Church that they sent for Jacob Creath, Sr., a prominent Baptist preacher, to come and win him back. Jacob Creath appealed to the Gano family history and how his beloved grandfather, the famous Baptist preacher, would have been disappointed. It is said that at that point, John Allen Gano laid his hand on the New Testament and said, "Elder Creath, if you will show me in this book where it says, "deny yourself, take up your cross and follow your grandfather, I will follow mine through life. But I read it, follow Christ, and I am determined to follow Him until death if it separates me from all the kindred I have on earth." Soon after this, Jacob Creath, Sr. became convinced that Gano had indeed made the right move, publicly renounced the Baptist religion, and took his stand with the church that had no book or creed.

John Allen Gano

From that time until the time of his death, John Allen Gano preached the gospel in the Georgetown region of Kentucky. His time was split between four churches: Leesburg, where he preached for fifty-nine years; Old Union, for fifty-five years; Newtown, from its inception in 1857, until his death in 1887; and Antioch, the number of years of service not being known. W. C. Morro, in an address at the Georgetown Cemetery on September 26, 1909, said that John Allen Gano baptized almost 15,000 persons.

Richard M. Gano, obviously, was an admirer of his father and patterned his life after him. He wrote of his father in John T. Brown's, <u>Churches of Christ</u>, 1904 edition:

> [A]n able defender of the truth, a close adherent to God's Word, a remarkable exhorter, and his life came up so closely to his preaching that his influence was great, and he could quiet discordant elements to a remarkable degree, and was often called many miles to make peace between men. As a neighbor, a husband, a father, he was hard to excel, and was looked up to and held up as an example as far as he was well known, and his name and memory are

cherished by a host of friends. His liberality was proverbial, both to the church and to the world, and his success in business was so remarkable that he amassed a goodly amount of property, not withstanding his charities, and liberal provisions for a large family; and his untiring labors in the Master's vineyard, helping to build churches, and contributing liberally to missionary work.

General Richard Gano

This background information brings us to subject of this story, General Richard Montgomery Gano, CSA. Born in 1830, Richard was the second child of John Allen and Mary Catherine Gano. He was an intelligent child, and entered Bacon College at the age of twelve, and completed his course of study at Bethany College in 1847, at the age of seventeen. He graduated medical school at the Louisville Medical School two years later in 1849.

Dr. Gano practiced medicine in Kentucky and Louisiana, but moved to Texas, which was to become his adopted state. In 1859, Gano moved to Grapevine Prairie, Texas, on the site of the present day Dallas/Fort Worth International Airport. His interest in farming and producing the best stock helped the young doctor to amass wealth. He was actively involved in community affairs and when the community was attacked by hostile Indians, Gano organized and led troops against them. For his leadership, the community demonstrated their appreciation by presenting to him a sword.

Dr. Gano was also very active in the local church. His activities in the community, church, farming community, and as the local doctor, earned him the respect of his neighbors. He was elected to the Texas State legislature in 1860.

When the Civil War broke out, Richard Gano resigned his seat in the Legislature in early 1861 and organized the "Grapevine Volunteers," a company of riflemen. He was chosen as their captain. By July 1862, Gano was serving under Colonel John Hunt Morgan's 2nd Kentucky Calvary in

Chattanooga, Tennessee. In September 1862, Gano's squadron became the nucleus of the 7th Kentucky Cavalry Regiment, and Gano was promoted to the rank of Colonel. He participated in a number of campaigns, and after General John Hunt Morgan was killed, he assumed command of Morgan's survivors and continued to command his own troops. Gano and these soldiers were placed under the command of General Nathan Bedford Forrest and fought with him at the Battle of Chickamauga.

One of the most interesting battles of the Civil War was at Chickamauga, where gospel preachers on opposite sides were engaged in the battle. These were General James A. Garfield, USA, and General Richard M. Gano, CSA. As one thinks of this match-up of opposing Christians and gospel preachers, one might think also of how many Christians were involved in the Civil War and wonder how many Christians killed Christians on the other side in the name of their country?

Even in the Gano family there was great division. General Richard M. Gano's cousin was the Union General, Stephen Gano Burbridge. In 1864, Burbridge was given command over the state of Kentucky to deal with the growing problem of Confederate guerrilla campaigns. He established martial law as authorized by President Abraham Lincoln. On July 16, 1864, Burbridge issued Order No. 59 which declared:

> [W]henever an unarmed Union citizen is murdered, four guerrillas will be selected from the prison and publicly shot to death at the most convenient place near the scene of the outrages. During Burbridge's rule in Kentucky, he directed the execution and imprisonment of numerous people, including public figures, on charges of treason and other high crimes, many of which were baseless (wikipedia.org/wiki/Stephen _G._ Burbridge).

This action earned General Stephen Gano Burbridge the nickname, "Butcher of Kentucky."

On October 3, 1863, Gano assumed command of the Texas Cavalry, operating in the Trans-Mississippi Department. One of the most daring attacks of the war took place in Indian Territory at the Second Battle of Cabin Creek near Fort Smith, Arkansas, in July 1864. General Gano and General Stand Watie (the only Indian General in the Civil War) led a daring raid against a Federal supply train and captured three hundred wagons and 750 mules along with their supplies. The value of these was estimated at more than $2,000,000.00. General Kirby Smith called this "one of the most brilliant raids of the entire war."

Gano was promoted to the rank of Brigadier General, but did not receive the official notice until March 1865. General Gano was recommended for promotion to Major General, but the war ended before this could be acted upon.

General Richard Montgomery Gano was one of the South's most successful military officers. He participated in more than seventy battles, winning all but four of them. He had five horses shot out from under him during the course of the war.

General Gano was remembered by his troops as a man with deep personal interest in the spiritual welfare of all with whom he served. Perhaps because of his contact with the troops as a general, a doctor, and a preacher, he became one of the most beloved commanders of the entire army. Gano never forgot the men who served for the Southern cause, and for many years after the war, even into old age, Gano made appearances at many Civil War reunions.

After the war, General Gano returned to Kentucky where he was ordained to preach by Winthorp Hobson of the Old Union church, where his father, John Gano, preached most of his life. Over the next six years, General Gano would preach at Mount Carmel, Berea, Dry Run, Oxford, Cane Ridge, Stamping Ground, and Leesburg, Kentucky. In 1873, Gano moved back to Dallas County, Texas, where he continued to preach, farm, raise prize stock, and establish churches. In 1875, he served as a preacher in Dallas, but from 1876 until 1908, he traveled from place to place conducting protracted meetings lasting from one week to three months. The typical meeting would last one month. He traveled throughout Texas, Kansas, Missouri, Tennessee, and Kentucky preaching the gospel.

A Religious Conservative

General Gano was a conservative at a time when being a progressive was popular. In July 1886, a state meeting was held in Austin, Texas, for the purpose of the forming a missionary society. The delegates were evenly split, and the chairman voted in favor of the missionary society. The conservative preachers, General Gano, J. A. Clark, Carroll Kendrick, C. M. Wilmeth, W. H. D. Carrington, and others were ruled out of order by the chairman and not allowed to voice their opposition to the plan (Eckstein, History of the Churches of Christ In Texas, p. 238).

General Gano not only opposed the missionary society, he also opposed instrumental music in worship, which had become popular in many churches of Christ. General Gano was scheduled to hold a gospel meeting in Commerce, Texas, in August 1900. When an announcement was made in April of that year that the conservative preacher, General Gano would be holding the meeting, the progressives locked the door of the building so that the conservatives could not use the building on Sundays. However, the conservatives regained the building and changed the locks. This swapping of the building continued many times until finally the progressives allowed the conservatives to have the building.

Later Years

In his later years, General Gano served as an elder at the Pearl and Bryan church, along with A. T. Sitz and William

Lipscomb. On the night of July 10, 1899, James S. Dunn was holding a gospel meeting at this church when William Lipscomb, one of the elders and nephew of David Lipscomb, was shot to death during the service. General Gano's son, Maurice, apprehended the assailant and held him until the police came. Earl West gives this account of the tragedy in volume 3 of his book, The Search for the Ancient Order:

> Professor Lipscomb with his wife and four children sat on the front pew listening to the sermon. Behind them sat Maurice Gano, General R. M. Gano's bachelor-son-lawyer. The curtains leading from the baptismal room moved; a man stepped up to the front seat beside Professor Lipscomb, pulled out a revolver and shot him in the breast. Lipscomb leaped up, grabbed his chest and fell to the floor. Maurice Gano grabbed the assailant by the throat and held him for the police while Lipscomb's hysterical wife pillowed the head of her unconscious husband on her lap.

Lipscomb had served as the principal of Dallas Central High School. The assailant was a former janitor, John T. Carlisle, who had been fired from the school.

As he grew older, General Gano traveled less and stayed home more. He devoted more time to his business and to serving as an elder at the Pearl and Bryan church. General Gano's business interests were very profitable and allowed him to donate more money to missionary work. His interest in improving stock bloodlines continued as he imported better bloodlines into Texas, including cattle, thoroughbred horses, sheep, and hogs. He formed a real estate company and served as Vice-President of the Estado Land and Cattle Company. He also served as a Director of the Bankers and Merchants National Bank in Dallas. General Gano became very wealthy from these endeavors and donated millions of dollars to missionary work and left an inheritance of over a million dollars to his heirs at the time of his death (DeVries, Edward, The Christian Generals, p. 31).

General Gano died on March 27, 1913 at his home on the corner of Cedar Springs and Oaklawn Avenue in Dallas, Texas. He is buried in the Dallas Oakland Cemetery. David Lipscomb wrote of his death in the *Gospel Advocate*, May 1913: "General Gano was gentle and suave in his manner, but firm in his convictions and steadfast in his purposes." Lipscomb recounted he became well acquainted with General Gano during a gospel meeting. Lipscomb said, "I used to boast sometimes of abstemious habits; that I had never drunk a cup of coffee, smoked a cigar, or took a chew of tobacco or a drink of spirits as a beverage. I told this to the general. If I mistake not, he added that he never had drunk a cup of tea, in addition to my restraints."

In Dallas, three of General Gano's sons formed the law firm of Gano, Gano, and Gano. The oldest of General Gano's sons was William Beriah Gano. He received his law degree from Harvard. William's daughter, Allene Gano, married Howard Robard Hughes, Sr. Their son, Howard Hughes, Jr., became the wealthiest man in America and one of the wealthiest men in the world. He was known as a movie producer and director, developer of experimental aircraft, and held a number of aviation speed records. He owned Hughes Tool Company, Hughes Aircraft Company, and Trans World Airlines. Howard Hughes died in 1976, leaving a multi-billion dollar estate. His closest living relative was his aunt, Annette Gano Lummis. Her son, Will Lummis, an attorney, was chosen to handle the multi-faceted estate of Howard Hughes, which was made of several companies and many assets in different forms. This settling of the Hughes estate took many years.

The Legacy of Richard Gano

General Richard Montgomery Gano was not only a soldier in the Confederate army, he was a soldier of the cross of Jesus Christ. His personal journal records that from 1866 to 1908, he preached regularly in 13 different churches.

Between 1866 and 1883, he held 167 protracted meetings. The journal also records names, dates, and locations of 4,635 people that he baptized during the course of his ministry (Edward DeVries, p. 29). Another source says, "It is estimated that he personally baptized (immersed) 10,000 souls (http://members.aol.com/swarren385/cabincreek/gano.htm).

Earl West said, "By the time he (Gano) was eighty-one years old, he had baptized 6,800 people" (West, Search for the Ancient Order, vol. 3, p. 148). Still another source said "Before his death, the general was credited with 'saving sixteen thousand fellow Texans'" (Bartlett and Steele, Empire, The Life, Legend, and Madness of Howard Hughes, p. 29). Regardless of the number of baptisms, from these sources we can see that General Gano was obviously involved in several thousand conversions. General Gano and his father, John Allen Gano, were perhaps the only father and son to have each baptized as many as 10,000 people.

Dr. John Dwyer, Professor of History at Southern Nazarene University, wrote a foreword in Dr. Edward DeVries book, The Christian Generals, Vol. 3. He had this to say of Richard Gano:

> For a Texan of course, it (this book) resurrects the life and legacy of one of our greatest heroes, and causes us to wonder how we ever forgot him.
>
> For the American Indian, it shows the electrifying feats of which his ancestors were capable, such as when Gano's colleague in command, Cherokee General Stand Watie, and his Oklahoma Indian horse soldiers rode to thundering victory alongside the soft-spoken... preacher in the middle of the night at Cabin Creek.
>
> For the young single woman, Richard Gano is a reminder to wait on God's best, that He is in the business of raising up devout, pure, and faithful Christian men, in every generation, even when fools and blackguards surround them on every side.

For the young man (and those of us not-so-young), Gano, like no small number of other Confederate heroes, leaves a standard of immovable loyalty to our Saviour, albeit nurtured in graceful humility, which helps us remember—and gives us hope—that an honorable and chaste earthly pilgrimage is indeed possible for us.

Dr. Lawrence L. Anderson said of Gano, "The life and ministry of Brigadier General Richard Montgomery Gano was a powerful example of bravery, compassion, and devotion to God." Indeed, Richard Gano was one of the great personalities of the restoration movement and worked to preserve the church of the New Testament. David Lipscomb concluded the obituary of Richard Gano by saying, "The last years of this life he served as an elder in the church at Dallas, Texas and died respected and honored by those who knew him."

Chapter 17

From Preacher to President

James Abrams Garfield began his career as a gospel preacher and ended it as president of the United States. He is the only preacher to have ever served as president. He is the only sitting member of the House of Representatives to ever serve as president. He is the only Senate elect, non-seated member of the senate to ever serve as president.

James A. Garfield was a brilliant man. His intellect allowed him to succeed where most men would not. Without

James Garfield

military training, he became at the age of thirty, the youngest general in the United States, at the age of thirty-one, was advanced in rank to major general, and hailed as a hero of the war before leaving for Congress. He was a preacher, college president, attorney, member of the Ohio Senate, military leader, U. S. Representative, U. S. Senator, and President of the United States before dying at the relatively young age of forty-nine. His accomplishments are nothing short of amazing.

Garfield's Early Life

James Abram Garfield was born in a log cabin (the last of the log cabin presidents) on November 19, 1831, in Orange Township on the Western Reserve (now Ohio). His parents were Abram and Eliza Garfield. They had settled in this sparsely populated land, and Abram and Eliza Garfield were converted to New Testament Christianity by a Disciple preacher named Murdock. However, it was not until

Adamson Bentley moved to their neighborhood that the Garfields became active members of the church. Bentley had been converted by Alexander Campbell to the idea of the restoration of the New Testament Church. On January 22, 1833, Abram Garfield was immersed into Christ. Less than two weeks later, Eliza was baptized. Abram and Eliza's time together would be short. Abram died in May 1833, leaving Eliza to raise four young children. (James was only eighteen months old at the time.) This event moved Eliza closer to her religion. She became an avid Bible reader. She read it to her children and walked each Sunday with her children to the church meetinghouse three miles away. Time and again, she heard Bentley or another preacher plead for the restoration and union of all on the basis of the New Testament. Young James Garfield would never forget his early religious training.

James Garfield obeyed the gospel in a protracted meeting held by W. A. Lillie that ran from February 17th to March 1, 1850. Garfield wrote in his journal, "I was buried with Christ in baptism and arose to walk in newness of life." Seven months after his conversion to Christ, Garfield wrote:

> Two years ago I had become ripe for ruin. On the canal…ready to drink in every species of vice, and with the ultimate design of going on the ocean… I was taken sick; unable to labor, went to school two terms thus cultivating my moral and intellectual faculties, took a school in the winter and greatest of all, obeyed the gospel. Thus by the providence of God I am what I am and not a sailor. I thank Him.

As a boy, James had to work to help support his impoverished family. James worked on the canals, pulling boats (which required a great amount of strength) and cutting wood, doing the work of a man. When healthy, James was good at physical labor and was quite strong. He claimed he could chop two cords of wood a day. (This would be a 4' x 4' x 16' stack of wood.) He often came into contact with men of less than desirable behavior, but he held fast to his Christian morals.

James dreamed of leaving home and becoming a sailor, but his mother and his illness (malaria) changed his ambitions. His convalescence from malaria provided an opportunity for schooling.

Garfield's mother was concerned about James receiving an education, and at the very young age of three, James was attending classes in a nearby log hut, learning to read and developing a love of reading that broadened his education throughout his life. In 1849, Garfield's mother persuaded him to enter Geauga Academy in Chester, Ohio, about ten miles from the Garfield home. After his first term, he was able to earn enough money to become self supporting. He was described as a physical specimen of young manhood and of having an intellectual superiority. While at Geauga Academy, James met Lucretia Rudolph, his future wife, whom he married nine years later.

In 1851, after finishing his studies at Geauga Academy, Garfield entered Hiram Eclectic Institute (later Hiram College). Hiram College had its beginning when the Board unanimously elected Amos Sutton Hayden as Principal of the seminary. A disciple preacher, A. S. Hayden had obeyed the gospel through the teaching of Walter Scott, who immersed him in baptism on March 20, 1828. At the time, Hayden was fifteen years old. Hiram College became known as a "Disciples school," and there Garfield learned more of the faith that he was to carry with him throughout his life.

After his studies at Hiram, Garfield determined to continue his education. Working to save money for college, he selected Yale, Brown, and Williams College as the final three. He selected Williams College, and entered in the fall of 1854, and was graduated with highest honors in 1856. There Garfield's education was broadened. One area in which he excelled was debate. This would prepare him for later in life, especially for congressional service. He left

Williams College with an enviable record of public speaking, debate, and scholarship.

On returning to Ohio after graduation, he became a teacher of Latin and Greek at Hiram College. It is said of Garfield that he could take a pen in each hand and write in Latin and Greek simultaneously. Garfield could discuss any number of disciplines including science, religion, education, and art. His influence as an educator grew, especially among his students. As in all other aspects of life, Garfield was a successful teacher.

It was during this time that Garfield turned to preaching. Finding that he was comfortable preaching and having success in the conversion of souls brought delight, not only to Garfield but to the disciples in that area. Garfield held a number of protracted meetings in which many obeyed the gospel. One of these meetings was held in 1858 in Hiram, resulting in thirty-four baptisms. His popularity as a preacher and public speaker on non-religious subjects grew as those around Hiram realized the powerful figure that James A. Garfield was becoming.

At the age of twenty-six, Garfield became president of Hiram College. His influence as an educator brought about invitations to speak at teachers' meetings at various places. His ability as an administrator grew also, preparing him for the war years that were in the not so distant future. Garfield would hold this position as President of Hiram College until he resigned it to volunteer for the war.

During this time, Garfield studied to take the bar exam. In 1858, he entered his name as a student in a law office in Cleveland, but he studied at Hiram. It was typical at this time to "read law" as a way of learning the law and to do so under the supervision of an attorney. Many close to Garfield were not aware that he was "reading law." He completed his studies and was admitted to the bar before leaving Hiram.

On November 11, 1858, he married Lucretia Rudolph, and they had seven children. The last of these children to die was Abram, who died in 1958.

Garfield, the Military Leader

On July 27, 1861, Governor William Dennison, Jr., governor of Ohio, wrote Garfield, "I am organizing some new regiments. Can you take a lieutenant-colonelcy? I am anxious you should do so. Reply by telegraph." On July 16, 1861, Garfield reported for duty and received his commission. During this time, he raised a regiment of students from Hiram, many who were disciples. The transformation from citizen to soldier was not immediate. As Garfield said, "the fabric of my life is being demolished and reconstructed, to meet the new condition of affairs." First, Garfield had to learn the tactics and study books on military science. Next, he had to teach his officers these new found arts of war. At night, Garfield studied, perhaps harder than ever before. For days, weeks, and months, he pored over the subject of warfare. He gave himself a crash course in military science, learning tactics and strategies of an aspect of life he had never known. The advantage Garfield had over others was intellect and the ability to act on that intellect.

Assigned to General Don Carlos Buell on December 15, 1861, Buell showed Garfield a map of Kentucky and asked one question—"How shall the Confederate forces be chased out of Kentucky?" Garfield stayed up all night studying documents and information, and the next morning he submitted his plan for the campaign. On December 17, 1861, an order was issued from Buell to Garfield apprising him of the acceptance of Garfield's battle plan. On receipt of Buell's instructions, Garfield began instantly to carry them out. His plan worked as expected, and on January 10, 1862, Garfield's forces at the Battle of Middle Creek drove the confederates, under the command of Brigadier General Humphrey Marshall, from Kentucky.

This campaign was significant because it was the first Union victory of the war. The confidence of the North in its military leaders had begun to waver. Not only was General

Buell elated at Garfield's victory, the news of a Union victory was celebrated in Washington. President Lincoln was thrilled to finally have a victory. The South was astonished at Garfield's victory, and the North once again had reason to believe in itself. Garfield was commissioned a Brigadier General, dated back to January 10, 1862.

After the Battle of Middle Creek, Garfield returned to Louisville. He found that Buell was away in Columbia, Tennessee, and he left to meet up with him. Buell had made his way to Savannah, Tennessee, near Pittsburg Landing on the Tennessee River. Here forces were gathering for one of the great battles of the war, the Battle of Shiloh. Garfield reached Buell on April 7th, the second day of fighting, and participated in the battle. The Confederates retreated to Corinth, Mississippi. Under the command of General Henry W. Halleck, the General-in-Chief of all Union armies, the Union Army proceeded to Corinth at a snail's pace, taking six weeks to march thirty miles. Garfield referred to the march in pursuit of the Confederates as a disgrace. Two months later on June 25th, writing from Tuscumbia, Alabama, Garfield wrote a friend:

> After the evacuation of Corinth (an event which I am compelled to regard as disgraceful to our generalship) the Army of the Ohio immediately began to repair the Memphis and Charleston Railroad and since that time my brigade has been hard at work marching and building up bridges where one army or the other had burned them. I have for the past ten days been serving as the President of a General Court Martial and several of my regiments have gone on to repair the road eastward. I start to join them tomorrow morning at 3 o'clock and so I take a few moments of the evening before to write to you. In about three days I hope [to reach] Decatur, Alabama and I presume we shall go thence to Eastern Tennessee to liberate the Union men there from the terrible bondage which they have suffered.

In this letter, Garfield also tells of an order from his commanding general to have his men search for a fugitive slave. He writes:

> Not long ago my commanding general sent me an order to have my camp searched for a fugitive slave. I sent back word that if generals wished to disobey an express law of Congress, which is also an order from the War Department, they must do it themselves for no soldier or officer under my command should take part in such disobedience. We have marched scores of miles past splendid plantations waving with corn which the planters boast openly is intended to feed the Southern army. While masters and master's sons are away in the rebel army, the slaves under the whip of their driver toil on in the fields we are passing and dare hardly look up at us.

Garfield was probably referring to an order by General Henry W. Halleck, issued on November 20, 1861, directing the exclusion of slaves from within Union lines because of reports of slaves feeding information to the Confederates. A storm of criticism descended on the General for this order, who defended his order by saying it was military, not political. Garfield's response shows his knowledge of the law and of military matters. Garfield would protect (or at least, refuse to search for and apprehend) a slave, ignore an order from a superior officer, and the risk of a court martial and death, rather than search for the slave under question. Garfield was very sympathetic to the slaves, and on many occasions voiced his disgust at that "peculiar institution."

From Tuscumbia, Garfield went to Decatur, Alabama, also on the Memphis and Charleston Railroad. From there, he wrote his wife, Lucretia. In this letter he addressed to "Dear Crete," Garfield tells of a return of his illness. He struggled with malaria for many years and was having constant bouts with diarrhea. Part of this letter is quoted.

Headquarters, 20th Brigade
In Camp Near Decatur, Alabama
July 5, 1862.

Dear Crete,

    I'm sorry to have to tell you that my health is not only not improving, but getting worse. I have kept hoping that each attack of my besetting disease would be the last, but it has lately returned with a vigor and stubbornness which I am quite unable to control. I had begun to regain strength and weight, was weighing 177 pounds, but the last week has run me down to 168, and I am suffering a good deal of pain as well as weakness. If I do not get better soon I shall get a sick leave to go as far as Cincinnati if not all the way home.

Garfield also mentioned to his wife that there was an interest in him running for Congress. He wrote:

    A number of people have written me about running for Congress this fall. I have not determined what to say about it, until I can learn more of the state of feeling throughout the district. I would, of course, rather be in Congress than in the army if there is to be no more active service, for I have no taste for the dull monotony of camp life, and then I believe I can dispose of my life to more advantage than to confine it to the inglorious quiet of a brigade camp. Still, I am very unwilling to do anything that would look like a desire to leave my place in the army, nor will I as long as my health will hold out. It is that which made me say I might go as far as Cincinnati, if I did not go clear through home, should I continue unwell very much longer. To go home just now would, I fear, be misconstrued into a purpose to make political capital for myself. I have been [so] thoroughly dead militarily since I came to the Tennessee that I hardly see how I can be sufficiently remembered to make my return a matter of much comment; still it might be, and I don't

[know] why it is, but I have a more than usual horror at being hauled over the coals of political persecution again. What do you hear said about the congressional matter?

Garfield's closing paragraph is of particular interest to restoration historians. He closes the letter with this information:

> Several Disciples of the vicinity have been here to visit me. There is a church in the village of Mooresville near by and they have sent up wanting me to speak to them on Sunday next. If I am not too unwell I have a notion to speak to them.
>
> I hope to hear from you again in regard to what you think about the matters referred to above. Love to all.
> Ever yours,
> James

Mooresville Church of Christ

The Church of Christ at Mooresville, Alabama, had its beginning when Dr. John H. Hundley was baptized into Christ for remission of sins in 1839 by Dr. Carroll Kendrick. The church met in homes until a house of worship was built in the little village of Mooresville.

The June 5, 1862 letter is the only record of Garfield speaking at the church of Christ in Mooresville, Alabama. However, oral history, passed down by members of the church at Mooresville, indicates that Garfield did indeed speak at the Mooresville church. This must have caused quite a stir at the Presbyterian Church located a block away. The church of Christ had managed to build a building in 1854 and by 1857 had added several members from the Presbyterian Church. This outraged the Presbyterian minister, and during a service, he pointed west toward the worship place of the church of Christ and said, the church of Christ down on the corner is "the egg of the devil, hatched in the mudsills of hell."

The invitation of a Union General to speak in the church was quite remarkable. The invitation was probably issued by Dr. J. H. Hundley, minister of the church in Mooresville. Hundley had three sons fighting for the Confederacy: one would not survive the war, the other two were captured and spent time at the Johnson Island Prison Camp in Ohio. Not only that, but in 1861, twenty-three year old Johnny Tucker, a member of the Mooresville church, had been killed in the war. Union soldiers camped near Mooresville had devastated the area around Mooresville and Athens, Alabama. So horrendous were the actions of these soldiers that their leader, Colonel John Turchin, was court martialed. General Garfield presided over the proceedings.

Colonel John Turchin was born Ivan Turchaninov in Russia and was trained in the Imperial Military School in St. Petersburg. In 1856, he immigrated to the United States and offered his services to the Union when the war broke out. Troops under Turchin sacked the little town of Athens, Alabama, even though it was populated by a pro Union population. Turchin, using the methods of war commonly practiced in Europe, allowed his men to destroy property, and a charge of raping a fourteen year old girl was brought up.

Garfield was selected as a judge in the court martial, and General Buell relieved Turchin of duty. However, before the court martial concluded, President Abraham Lincoln promoted Turchin to the rank of Brigadier General.

War had brought devastation, not only to the land, but the church. There was much bitterness on both sides. Not only did brother fight against brother, but brother in Christ fought against brother in Christ. But in July 1862, a Union General preached the gospel of Christ in a rebel church.

Shortly after preaching at Mooresville, Garfield returned home to recuperate from his illnesses. When his health improved, he went to Washington for four months to await an assignment. While there, Garfield wrestled with thoughts of either running for Congress or remaining in the army. He decided to place the question before the man who could probably feel more sympathy for him than anyone else. Abraham Lincoln, like Garfield, came from poverty. Lincoln thought Garfield's question over and finally said, "The Republican majority in Congress is very small, and it is often doubtful whether we can carry the necessary war measures; and, besides, we are greatly lacking in men of military experience in the House to regulate legislation about the army." Lincoln concluded, "It is your duty, therefore, to enter Congress, at any rate for the present." Lincoln reasoned it was easier to find generals than it was to get good congressmen.

Finally, Garfield received the assignment as the Chief of Staff for General William S. Rosecrans, who was involved in the Tullahoma Campaign in Central Tennessee. Rosecrans immediately learned to appreciate Garfield. His genius for tactics and planning were obvious. His reports were detailed and flawless. Garfield and Rosecrans made a connection religiously. Rosecrans, a devout Catholic, and Garfield, a member of the church of Christ, would stay awake until the early morning hours discussing religion.

Garfield had a great admiration for Rosecrans. In a letter to Lucretia dated January 26, 1863, Garfield said of Rosecrans:

> I am, however, greatly pleased with some features of General Rosecrans' character. He has that fine quality of having his mind made up on all the great

questions which concern his work. In a military man this is a cardinal virtue."

He added:

> General Rosecrans thinks rapidly and strikes forward into action with the utmost confidence in his own judgement. In this he is perfectly unlike McClellan, who rarely has a clear-cut, decisive opinion, and dare[s] not trust it when he has.
> There is much in his appearance that is striking and singular… He carries a cross attached to his watch dial, and as he drew his watch out of his side-pants pocket his rosary, a dirty looking string of friars beads, came out with it.

Garfield was delighted to learn more about the Catholic religion from Rosecrans. Rosecrans also had a great influence on Garfield's thinking, and some may have believed that Garfield temporarily professed Catholicism, or at least was greatly influenced to accept Catholicism. This speculation is due to a letter by Garfield to his mother on March 22, 1863. From Murfreesboro, Tennessee, Garfield wrote:

> [The] principal church in this place is owned by the Disciples. It is a very large, fine building, and there was before the war a flourishing congregation; but the minister was a rebel and is now a chaplain in the rebel army and the church is scattered. The building is now used as a hospital.

Garfield went on to say, "General Rosecrans has Catholic service in his room or mine every few days. I sometimes attend and as I can understand the Latin service it is not altogether unmeaning to me." In light of the Disciples not meeting and Rosecrans holding religious services which Garfield attended, Garfield wrote to his wife, saying, "I hope you are not alarmed about my becoming a Catholic. You ought to be glad that I take time to think and talk about religion at all."

It seems from the context of the letter that Garfield was not espousing Catholicism, but that it appeared he was a Catholic because he could not meet with the Disciples, and the worship he attended with Rosecrans provided the only worship service available.

Union plans were made to take Chattanooga. This was accomplished, but on the southern side of Lookout Mountain, in the center of the valley, ran a little river called Chickamauga. The Confederates were camped on the south side of this stream. Although Garfield answered to Rosecrans, it was Garfield who developed the plans for the Battle of Chickamauga. He knew the positions of all the commanders, army strength, and location of artillery. Every division commander obeyed orders from headquarters, took his position, and fought. From his headquarters, Garfield issued every order and every change of order. Notes of slips of white paper were incessantly written by General Garfield and handed to aides who immediately galloped away to the recipients. Soon, messengers begin to arrive at headquarters with reports of the battle. Garfield made all decisions, calling up reinforcements and changing positions as the battle progressed. Garfield's orders were well written, clear, in unmistakable English, and understandable without question. They did not contain a doubtful phrase or misplaced comma. Every officer understood and executed what was expected of him. Garfield knew every movement, every position, and had a perfect comprehension of the situation of the troops.

On the second day of the battle, an aide galloped to headquarters and informed General Rosecrans that there was a chasm in the center between the divisions of General Reynolds on the left and General Wood on the right. In the excitement of the crisis, Rosecrans, failing to consult with Garfield, who was deeply involved in another matter, issued an order for General Wood to close up on Reynolds as fast as possible and support him. Had only Rosecrans consulted Garfield, he would have been told that General Brannan's division was between Wood and Reynolds. This fatal order of battle was the only one that Garfield did not write himself. Wood was confused. He could not close up on Reynolds because Brannan was in the way. Wood, therefore marched his division backward, passed to the rear of Brannan, and thus to the rear of and support of Reynolds. The result was a breach in the line and eventual rout of the Union Army. In an attempt to save men and reorganize the army, General Rosecrans rode to Chattanooga to reassemble the army and General Garfield rode to the front lines to warn General Thomas of the broken line.

As a result of the Battle of Chickamauga, the Confederates won the battle and extended the war, General William Rosecrans was relieved of duty, and General Garfield was advanced in rank to Major General. But this would be Garfield's last battle. He received a mandate from the people of Ohio to represent them in Washington. At the age of thirty-one, Garfield resigned his commission to take a job as a U. S. Representative.

Garfield, the Congressman

Politician seems to be a cheapened term for the office Garfield held in the U. S. House of Representatives for the next sixteen years of his life. Garfield was elected to Congress in October, 1862, while serving as a general in the U. S. army. He continued to serve in the army until Congress met in December, 1863. During this time, he was promoted to Major General after the Battle of Chickamauga. He resigned his commission, effective December 5, 1863, to take his seat in the House of Representatives. Financially, Garfield would receive half of the salary he would make as a major general. He was re-elected every two years, from 1864 through 1878.

According to W. W. Wasson's book, <u>James A. Garfield: His Religion and Education</u>, Garfield went to Washington and became an active member of the church. At the time, the church met in the home of Dr. James T. Barclay, the first minister of the church. Garfield supported the raising of funds to build a building for the church, but he died before the building was completed. He was partly responsible for bringing Henry T. Anderson to Washington as a minister. Garfield and Judge Jeremiah S. Black, another member of the church, worked to secure a government job for Anderson so he could have support while he preached. Throughout the 1870s, Garfield's journal included a number of annotations of attending services, and he seldom missed a service. Sometimes he would preach at the church, but spoke less as his congressional duties increased. Wasson said that when Garfield was elected president, he brought a national recognition and prestige to the church. He wrote:

> His election caused the American public to give more attention to this religious movement and though it was common knowledge among the Disciples, the unique feature of having as president a man who had at one time been a preacher of the gospel and a teacher of religion stirred the religious mind of the country and produced overly optimistic predictions for the cause of religion.

In 1880, James A. Garfield was elected the United States Senator from Ohio. Before his term began, he became involved in the presidential campaign of 1880.

In the 1880 presidential campaign, John Sherman, brother of General William Tecumseh Sherman, was considered the best choice for the Republican Party. However, the party could not muster enough votes for Sherman. Garfield entered his name as a presidential candidate, and on the thirty-sixth ballot, he was chosen as the Republican Party candidate. The Democratic nominee for president was General Winfield Scott Hancock. Garfield won the election by fewer than 2,000 popular votes, but he was able to garner 214 of the 369 electoral votes.

Garfield, the 20th President of the United States

Garfield resigned his other positions and, on March 4, 1881, took office as president. He never sat in the Senate to which he was elected because the term began on the same day he took office as president. In the four months Garfield served as president before the assassination attempt, he threw off the shackles of senatorial courtesy and strengthened and revitalized the office of the presidency. Garfield routed his political foes and showed that he was a president to be dealt with. He strengthened the Federal authority over the New York Customs House, which was a stronghold of Republican Senator Roscoe Conkling, and submitted a list of appointments to the Senate, nominating Conkling's arch rival, William H. Robertson, to run the Customs House. Conkling contested the nomination and tried to persuade the Senate to block it. Conkling failed, and Garfield won back respect to the presidency.

His presidency would be a short one. On July 2, 1881, Garfield went to the Washington railroad depot to catch a train for an appointment to speak at Hiram College. As Garfield proceeded through the station, Charles Guiteau, a disgruntled lawyer, shot Garfield twice, one bullet piercing his arm, the other his abdomen.

Guiteau had worked with the Republican National Committee and felt he was responsible for Garfield's election. He sought an ambassadorship for his assistance. His requests were continually rejected. On May 14, 1881, he was told never to return by James Blain, Secretary of State.

Guiteau decided to kill the ungrateful Garfield. He purchased a revolver with borrowed money. On July 2, after stalking the president for some time, he caught up with him at the Washington railroad station. After the shooting,

Guiteau was immediately arrested, tried for the murder of Garfield, and was hanged.

The doctors administering to Garfield made several mistakes in his treatment, inserting their unwashed fingers into the bullet hole, as they probed for the bullet. In an attempt to find the bullet, sixteen attending physicians prodded and groped his wound. Infection set in. Because of the hot summer in Washington, the decision was made to take Garfield to the New Jersey shore where it was cooler. Garfield's attendants even rigged up an air-conditioning system, using electric fans to blow over ice, cooling the president's room.

Dr. Alexander Graham Bell had invented a metal detector and it was used to experiment on the president to find the bullet. The metal detector gave a reading that the bullet was deep in Garfield's body. What they didn't know was the bed on which the president was placed had metal springs, something almost unheard of at the time. The metal detector was actually picking up the metal in the springs.

On the evening of September 16, James Abrams Garfield died with his wife, Lucretia, by his side.

Conclusion

There have been three Presidents of the United States with backgrounds and connections to the restoration movement. They were James A. Garfield, Lyndon B. Johnson, and Ronald W. Reagan. Only one of these men, Garfield, was a preacher. He understood the gospel plan of salvation and obeyed it from his heart. Garfield was a very brilliant man who for several years before the war preached the gospel and converted many to Christ.

Chapter 18

In Search of J. H. Hundley

The name, John Henderson Hundley, was unknown to me until a few years ago. At that time, I began a study of restoration history of churches of Christ. Through Wayne Kilpatrick's excellent article on the church of Christ at Mooresville, Alabama, I became aware of the name of J. H. Hundley.

Dr. J. H. Hundley

John Henderson Hundley was born in Halifax County, Virginia. He and Melinda Robinson were married in Greensville County, Virginia in September 1824. The Hundleys came to North Alabama from Virginia and settled in Madison County. Daniel Robinson, Melinda's father, was a merchant and a planter in Limestone County, Alabama. The Hundleys later moved to Limestone County and settled a short distance west of the little village of Mooresville, Alabama, on what would become known as Hundley Hill.

The Hundleys had six sons. They were Oscar, Orville, Daniel, Samuel, William, and John. Hundley was a physician, preacher, farmer, and at one time, a school teacher. Well educated and spiritually-minded, J. H. Hundley studied his Bible with an open mind to the teachings of the scriptures.

During his studies, Hundley came across a religious journal, *The Evangelist*, edited by Walter Scott of Kentucky. As a result of the truths taught in this journal, Hundley came to the conclusion that he had to be baptized for the remission of sins. He wrote Scott the following letter in 1840:

DEAR BROTHER SCOTT: The truth has taken a strong hold in this section; being last August convinced of the faith, I wrote to the brethren of Tuscumbia to send over a person to immerse me. Brother Kendrick came; he has for some time continued to teach us here the true gospel: the effect has been glorious: we now number seventy. To God be all the glory. Yours in the Lord, J. S. (sic,) HUNDLEY, Mooresville, Ala (*The Evangelist*, 1840, p. 113). [Note: typographical error. Should have been J. A. Hundley.]

In 1854, the church building at Mooresville was completed and the group that formerly met in the home of Dr. Hundley moved to the new building. Hundley preached for the church at Mooresville for many years. Hundley was the minister during the Civil War when General James A. Garfield preached there. The invitation for Garfield to preach probably came through Hundley, whose three sons fought for the Confederacy. They were William, who would be killed late in the war and Daniel and Orville, who survived the war. William and Daniel were both incarcerated in the Johnson Island prison camp in Ohio, and were there at the same time.

However, this story is not about J. H. Hundley, per say, but about searching for information about Hundley. Having read articles about the Mooresville church and Hundley, and having developed an interest in the man, the initial pursuit of Hundley was somewhat accidental.

In October 2006, I visited the little village of Mooresville, Alabama, with a group, including two restoration historians, Earl Kimbrough and Larry Whitehead, who were interested in the Mooresville church. After spending some time around the quaint little village—so beautiful and preserved that it really takes you back in time—we went to the Mooresville Restaurant for lunch, where we met the restaurant's owner. I asked her if she knew anyone who could give us information about the Hundley family. She told me she knew someone and would make arrangements for us to talk over the phone.

She also produced a photograph of the Hundley home, which once stood across the street from her home and was just north of the Mooresville church building. Just the picture alone was a great find, but what was to follow was even greater. I learned that a local historian could answer many of my questions about the Hundley family.

Meeting Jacque over the phone was a delightful experience. Her interest in and knowledge of Madison County, Alabama history and her family—the Hundley family—was to open doors for me. Jacque is a descendant of Dr. J. H. and Melinda Robinson Hundley, descending through their son, William. Jacque's willingness to share information with me was a joy. Not only did she have a picture of the Hundleys (which was one of the points of my search), she had something else. Wayne Kilpatrick had told me years ago that Hundley had written a book called the Plan of Salvation, published in 1858. As Jacque and I were talking, she said, "I also have a book that J. H. Hundley wrote." Excitedly, I asked, "Is it a small book with about eighty pages about the gospel plan of salvation?" "Yes," she replied. "Is there any way I can get a copy of it?" "Sure," said Jacque, "I'll make you a copy and send it to you." We continued our conversation until it was necessary to conclude, and I made arrangements to meet Jacque the first week in November when I was scheduled to preach in a gospel meeting at the Jordan Park Church of Christ in Huntsville, Alabama. During that period, we emailed each other a number of times, me asking for information and Jacque willingly supplying it.

When I received the copy of J. H. Hundley's, Plan of Salvation, I immediately made a copy and took it to Heritage Christian University to give it to Wayne Kilpatrick. Wayne, who seldom gets excited, gleamed when I gave him his copy of Hundley's work. Wayne returned to his classroom, and as I was leaving, I heard him tell his class, "I have just been given a book for which I have searched thirty years." I smiled and I walked away with the feeling of "mission accomplished." I finally was able to do something for the man who had introduced me not only to J. H. Hundley but also to the study of restoration history. It was Wayne who set me on my journey that led back to him with this document.

It was the first week in November when I met Jacque. An unusually warm fall day, the colorful leaves were still on the trees at the Maple Hill Cemetery in Huntsville, where Jacque showed me around. There we saw the Hundley plot and the graves of Dr. J. H. Hundley, his wife, Melinda, several children, and other family members. After talking to Jacque on the phone and corresponding by email, meeting her in person was great. She had been a tremendous help in the search for J. H. Hundley.

Another thing that Wayne Kilpatrick had mentioned to me about Hundley was that he had been told of a portrait of Hundley with his book in the portrait. Again, I emailed Jacque and asked her if she knew of such a portrait. She wrote back telling me that a great-grandson of J. H. Hundley was still alive, that he lived in New Market, Madison County, Alabama, and that he might be in possession of the elusive portrait. Jacque gave me his address. From the address, I looked up his phone number on the computer, found it, and made a call to Mr. McCrary, great-grandson of J. H. Hundley. I talked with McCrary's daughter, Rosemary. She was very cordial and willing to help in any possible way. She told me her father did have the portrait, and that it hung in the hallway of their home for many years. Arrangements were made to travel to New Market to meet Mr. McCrary, son of Mary Hundley, the daughter of J. H. and Melinda Hundley of Mooresville, Alabama.

On December 4, 2006, Larry Whitehead, Wayne Kilpatrick, and I traveled to New Market, Alabama to meet Mr. McCrary. Mr. McCrary was ninety-five years old and a picture of health. He had no wrinkles in his face and went to his farm everyday to work. He and his wife and their daughter, Rosemary, were so sweet to help us in any possible way. We were allowed to take the portrait of Dr. Hundley outside in the natural light to make photographs. Thomas showed us his grandfather's Bible that was published in 1858—the same year Hundley wrote The Plan of Salvation. We scanned several documents into the computer for later reference and talked with the McCrarys.

One of the stories Thomas told was about attending the Mooresville church of Christ as a boy and being in his Aunt Hattie Hundley's Bible class. As Miss Hattie was teaching, the boys in the class noticed a calf had wandered into the churchyard and toward the outhouse. The calf pushed open the door of the outhouse and went inside and turned around as though it was going to use the outhouse. The boys found this to be quite hilarious and broke into laughter. After the class, Miss Hattie went to one of the men, a brother Peebles, and told him that she didn't think she could teach class anymore.

During this search for J. H. Hundley, Bobby Graham from Athens, Alabama, mentioned to Larry Whitehead that Quentin McCay, an elderly North Alabama preacher had preached at the Mooresville church of Christ in the 1940s, and perhaps could give us some information about the church and the Hundley family. We met with brother McCay, and he shared his story about Mooresville. I taped the interview and transcribed it. Brother McCay told of being a college student at Freed-Hardeman College in the early 1940s and coming home on the weekends and preaching for the Mooresville church. He remembered some of the old members of the church and provided us with a picture of Hattie Hundley, grand-daughter of J. H. and Melinda Hundley, who on many occasions provided Sunday dinner for him after worship services. Brother McCay died shortly after this interview.

At this point in the search for J. H. Hundley, many questions had been asked and answered. However, with each bit of information, new questions arise, requiring more research. It is a never ending process, like finding the "missing pieces of the puzzle" and then learning that the puzzle is bigger than originally thought.

Another piece of this puzzle was the discovery of a journal written by Colonel Daniel Hundley, CSA, son of J. H. and Melinda Hundley. Several weeks of research on the computer put me in touch with Dr. Rex Miller, who edited the journal and published it. I was able to secure three copies of Daniel Hundley's journal from Dr. Miller. Daniel kept the journal of his capture and time served in the Johnson Island, Ohio, prison camp. The journal is a most insightful look into the life of a civil war prison camp. It tells of near starvation treatment as well as near freezing conditions for the soldiers.

Daniel Hundley was graduated from the Harvard School of Law and he soon after married the daughter of a Virginia gentleman, largely interested in real estate in the suburbs of Chicago. Hundley moved to Chicago in 1856 and owned a large amount of property on the lake shore, just north of the (then) city limits of Chicago. Daniel enjoyed Chicago and planned to make it his permanent home. However, the war broke out, and he said, "I unhesitating cast in my lot with the people of my native State" (Alabama).

Hundley escaped Johnson Island on January 2, 1865, and "attempted to reach Canada afoot, walking at night and sleeping in the hay-lofts during the day." He was recaptured, and taken back to Johnson Island, and stripped to the skin. His journal was found and confiscated. Nine years were to go by before he heard what happened to the journal. In 1874, he received a notice from the Postmaster in Huntsville, Alabama, that a certain Alexander R. Jones of New York desired his address. Hundley gave his address and soon received a letter from Mr. Jones telling him that he was acquainted with a man who had in his possession the journal Hundley had written while in prison. Mr. Jones thought he could purchase it for a reasonable sum and sell it to Hundley.

Daniel Hundley immediately wrote back telling Mr. Jones that he was too poor to purchase the journal and the honorable thing to do was to return the journal to him without payment, since it belonged to him anyway. The journal was received by Hundley shortly thereafter.

One of the interesting things mentioned in the journal was that Daniel Hundley's brother, William, was captured and sent to the same prison. It was when William arrived that Daniel received news about his family back in Mooresville, Alabama. William reported the following account of atrocities done to the Hundley family at Mooresville and Daniel recorded the account as follows:

> The blue-coated villains went to my father's house, one night last winter, entered my father's sleeping apartment, and ordered him, and (sic) old man of seventy years, to get up and leave, as they desired to search the house for gold; and upon his refusing to comply with their orders, ruffians drew a pistol and threatened to shoot him on the spot, which threat he doubtless would have carried into execution had not my mother that instant stepped between the would-be murderer and his helpless victim, and exclaimed, with a courage and nobility of soul which would have done honor to the matrons of old Rome in her best days: 'Then kill me, too, for the ball that kills my husband must first pass through my body!' The heroic defender of the old flag had no respect for the gray hairs of a feeble old man, but the dauntless courage of a resolute woman unnerved his coward's heart, and after robbing them of all he could put his hands on, he and his brother cut-throats left.

Research also yields information that Daniel Hundley was a resident of Mountain Home in the 1870's and was engaged in the practice of law. He would have, no doubt, been acquainted with J. M. Pickens who preached for the church at Mountain Home at that time, and the Barclay brothers, Robert G. and John Judson, who were closely associated with Pickens and lived nearby. The Barclay boys were the sons of James Turner Barclay, the first missionary of the American Christian Missionary Society, and they married Alexander Campbell's daughters. Judson married Decima Campbell, and Robert married Emma Campbell, adopted daughter of Alexander and Selina Campbell.

Another connection would be T. B. Larimore's connection to the Hundleys. T. B. Larimore performed the wedding ceremony for Daniel's daughter, Maude, in 1877. Records also show Larimore preaching at Mooresville. These families must have been close.

J. H. Hundley was born in 1796 and died in 1881. He lived a long and prosperous life. He had a great influence for good, working as a teacher, doctor, and gospel preacher. He was highly respected by those who knew him. His son, Daniel, wrote the following obituary that appeared in the Athens, Alabama newspaper:

> Died at his residence in Limestone county, ala., on the 3rd of January, 1881, Dr. JOHN H. HUNDLEY, being 85 years of age, lacking only a few weeks.
>
> Even the most loving of friends would fail to do justice to the memory of this faithful and venerable servant of God. After a long life of usefulness and labor, of good deeds and noble aspirations, loved and respected by all who knew him, and most by those who knew him best, he has been gathered to his fathers at last and now sleeps in the sleep of the just. It can be said of him in all sincerity, that, from his earliest youth up to the close of his long life, he was a model Christian gentlemen. In the days of his prosperity his land was as open as charity itself, and at all times his greatest joy was to visit the widows and the fatherless in their afflictions; and no man ever kept himself more unspotted from the world. He was an Israelite indeed in whom there was no guile. As a physician he was eminently successful, and the poor especially always found him a faithful friend. As a devoted and zealous minister of the gospel for more than thirty years, he won the hearts of all those who

came in contact with him. He never sought or would have received an compensation for his labor in the service of his Divine Master, on the contrary was ever liberal of his means in helping to build houses for Christian worship in places where the people were too poor to help themselves." As a father, and in all the domestic and social relations he was simply without a peer.

For quite a number of years he had been a confirmed invalid, and for the past three months a great sufferer. He bore his afflictions with Christian fortitude, waiting like the Apostle Paul, for the day of his departure; for like him he could truthfully say, "I have fought a good fight, I have finished my course, I have kept the faith; henceforth there is laid up for me a crown of righteousness, which the Lord, the righteous judge, will give him at that day (*The Alabama Courier*, February 17, 1881, p. 3.).

John Henderson Hundley was a man that was concerned about living as God would have him to live. This concern was not only for his personal well-being, but for the well-being of his family, friends, patients, and social contacts. He preached the gospel from 1834 until he became an invalid. We would do well to imitate his example.

Chapter 19

Memory of a Forgotten Infant

In May 2005, while walking through the Gresham Cemetery in Florence, Alabama, with restoration historians Wayne Kilpatrick and Earl Kimbrough, I heard from them for the first time the story of an infant buried there. The Gresham Cemetery is named for the family of Philemon Gresham, the father-in-law of Theophilus Brown Larimore, one of the most prominent gospel preachers of the late nineteenth and early twentieth centuries. The cemetery is the final resting place of many of Larimore's family and friends, including his first wife, Esther, son Toppie (Theophilus Brown Larimore, Jr.), and many of his Gresham in-laws. In the northwest corner of the cemetery is the grave of an infant girl, not related to the Larimores or Greshams. The grave is that of Mamie Srygley, the infant daughter of Fletcher Douglas Srygley and his wife, Ella Parkhill Srygley.

One needs only to walk through an old cemetery to become aware of the great number of infants and children who died in their youth in by gone years. The death of a child was a common tragedy before the advent of modern medicine and drugs that could cure childhood illnesses. In days past, the sneeze, wheeze, or cough of a small child was a sounding alarm for young parents. Such symptoms could signal the onset of an illness that could take the life of an infant or child and devastate a young family. One can only imagine the inconsolable grief of a young family as they buried an innocent child.

Before we relate the story of little Mamie Srygley, let us explore the reason why this little girl was buried in the Gresham cemetery.

In 1868, T. B. Larimore came to North Alabama to the Rock Creek church in the mountains of Franklin County (later to become part of the newly established Colbert County). At this time, Larimore was twenty-six years old, a Civil War veteran (who served as a Confederate spy), and after the war, obeyed the gospel and determined to become a gospel preacher. As the young preacher approached the Rock Creek building, he noticed a boy about thirty feet away. Larimore, recalling this occasion, gives the following description of the young boy he met that day:

> [T]he first time, I approached the door of that old log cabin meetinghouse, a penniless stranger in a strange land, I saw, standing about thirty feet away, to the right and front of me, twenty feet from the door I was approaching, a bright, little black-eyed, bareheaded, barefooted boy; a picture of health, happiness, peace, and contentment; perfectly beautiful to me then as, on memory's page, now. His cheeks were rosy; his eyes were black. Faultless in form and feature, he stood silent, motionless, and erect.
>
> He was standing there to see 'the preacher' as he passed, probably not caring to ever be nearer him than then. Instinctively I turned toward him, went to him, took his little right hand into mine, put my left arm around him, said something I deemed appropriate to him, and led him into the house. From that day to the day when, in the delirium of death, he, suddenly recognizing me, enthusiastically grasped me by both hands and thrilled my soul with an expression I can never forget, he was my devoted friend.

At this impromptu meeting, neither the boy nor Larimore could fathom the significance of the association that would develop between them. If there was ever a Paul/Timothy relationship in modern times, it was the relationship between Larimore and this young boy. The boy's name was Fletcher Douglas Srygley. In the relatively short life of F. D. Srygley (forty-three years), he would become an outstanding gospel preacher, front-page editor of the *Gospel Advocate*, and author of three books. Two of his most famous books were about his mentor, friend, and associate, T. B. Larimore.

F. D. Srygley attended Larimore's Mars Hill College in Florence, Alabama. By the time F. D. was seventeen years old, Larimore recognized Srygley's writing ability. This ability would serve him well in his life. Srygley admired his mentor, and as the boy grew to manhood, the two men became great friends with mutual admiration for each other's abilities. In the last quarter of the 19th century, Larimore became one of the most popular, if not the most popular, preacher in churches of Christ. It was during this time that Srygley, in his own right, became a well-known preacher and author. F. D.'s admiration for T. B. Larimore led him to write Smiles and Tears, Or Larimore and His Boys, a story about Larimore and his students at Mars Hill College. Over a hundred years later, the book is still widely read by those interested in church history. Srygley's last book, Letters and Sermons of T. B. Larimore, was completed shortly before his death.

F. D. Srygley died on August 2, 1900, just a few months shy of his forty-fourth birthday. He had been sick since his late twenties, suffering from Bright's disease (an archaic term for kidney disease). In fact, his brother, Filo Bunyon Srygley, said when F. D. married Miss Jennie Scobey (on December 26, 1888), "he was already an invalid and that she added ten years to his life." (Obviously Filo did not use the term invalid as we would use it, since F. D. continued to preach and write during this time and fathered five children by Jennie who survived him.)

Who else but T. B. Larimore could speak at the funeral of Fletcher Douglas Srygley? Larimore's oration, which appears in the August 30, 1900 issue of the *Gospel Advocate* (vol. XLII, p. 545), is pure Larimore, pure genius, the work of a wordsmith and scholar. In the eulogy, Larimore said:

When Stonewall Jackson fell, Lee, immortal hero of the lost cause, said: I have lost my right arm. Some of us, I am one, lost infinitely more than that when F. D. Srygley fell; and the cause that can never be lost, lost much more when our dear brother ceased to write, to talk, to breathe, than the lost cause lost when Stonewall Jackson said, 'Let us pass over the river and rest in the shade of the trees' and silently passed to the eternal shore.

F. D. Srygley

The eulogy was replete with expressions such as "beloved friend and brother," "my devoted friend," "faithful friend, than whom no human friend was ever truer," "my bosom friend," and "my constant correspondent a quarter of a century." Larimore said of Srygley, "with jealous care, (he) kept watch and ward over me, even as a brave, true husband shields and shelters the wife that he loves." Larimore said, "It is probable that no man on earth, even his own father not excepted, knew him more thoroughly or intimately than I."

It was in this funeral oration of Fletcher Douglas Srygley that Larimore recalled the event that took place twenty years before at Mars Hill, when Mamie, the infant daughter of F. D. and Ella Srygley, died. The young couple buried their firstborn in the Gresham Cemetery at Mars Hill, located four miles north of Florence, Alabama. F. D. was only twenty-three years old at the time of the death of his firstborn, and his wife was only eighteen years old. The young mother was overcome with grief and was inconsolable. Larimore relates the following story about this traumatic time in the life of Fletcher Douglas and Ella Parkhill Srygley.

To him and Ella were born two sweet little girls, Mamie and Jeffie. Before Jeffie was born, Mamie was taken from the cradle to the grave; was buried at Mars Hill, Ala., where the little family then lived.

Ella, the bereaved child mother, was inconsolable. Sighing and sobbing as if her aching heart would break, she said: 'O, if I had only kept one sweet little curl, one of the curls I loved so well and have so often kissed, how precious it would be to me now! But my baby is gone, all gone, and how can I live without her?'

The sun was sinking in the west, the day on which little Mamie was buried was nearly gone, when the thoughts of that sweet curl gave birth to that heartrending wail of woe. The Mars Hill school and community were a family filled with sympathy, confidence, and love then all glad to bear one another's burdens, and so fulfill the law of Christ.

Brother Srygley, his own heart bleeding and almost breaking, in strictest confidence submitted a strange suggestion to some of us. The mere suggestion was all sufficient. The sun set, the moon rose, the stars appeared, midnight came. The bereaved, childless mother slept. The stillness of death reigned supreme over the community. Little Mamie's grave was emptied; her little white coffin was opened. The sweetest curl that kissed her marble brow was clipped, a precious, tiny treasure for which the mother sighed. The coffin was closed and gently lowered into the grave; the grave was filled. At the proper time and in the proper way the curl was given to the mourning, moaning mother; but she never knew the story I have just revealed.

T. B. Larimore's description of the exhumation of the body of little Mamie Srygley at midnight forges images of several men by the light of an autumn moon and the light of lanterns using shovels to open the fresh grave of the little girl laid to rest only hours earlier. This was a task that none wanted, yet compelled by the grieving mother and suggestion of the father, the men accomplished the task before them.

Today, in the quietness of the Gresham Cemetery, the earthly remains of little Mamie Srygley, who was not quite thirteen months old when she died, rests in a small grave and waits the resurrection morning. A broken headstone silently watches over the infant's grave. Carved on the stone are these words:

MAMIE
Daughter of
F. D. & Ella P.
SRYGLEY
BORN
Sept. 29, 1879
DIED
Oct. 18, 1880
*"Suffer little children
to come unto Me"*

T. B. Larimore said that Ella Parkhill was "a sweet Christian girl, scarcely sixteen years old," when she and Fletcher Douglas Srygley married on December 22, 1878. He also said she made F. D. Srygley "a good, faithful, helpful, happy wife." Less than two years after F. D. and Ella were married, their firstborn child Mamie died. It seems that Ella was pregnant with their second child at the time and did not live long after the birth of Jeffie. Earl West wrote, "in a matter of a few months, she (Ella) followed her little girl to the grave" (West, <u>Search for the Ancient Order</u>, Vol. 3, p. 326).

It appears that Ella never recovered from the overwhelming grief of the death of her firstborn. Larimore stated in the funeral sermon for F. D. Srygley that Ella was buried in Savannah, Tennessee. F. D. Srygley suffered a double tragedy with the death of Mamie and Ella, and he was left with the responsibility of raising an infant girl,

Jeffie. Four years later, while in his mid-twenties, F. D. would become sick with a kidney disease that would affect him for the rest of his short life. At the time of Srygley's death, J. C. McQuiddy said, "his affliction was heart disease, which produced dropsy" (*Gospel Advocate*, August 9, 1900, p. 505). This is probably best described in today's term as congestive heart failure.

Grave of Mamie Srygley

Chapter 20

The Wedding That Never Happened

Perhaps there is not a more exciting time in the life of a young couple than their wedding day. Tom Allen and Mary Van Meter were very much in love. The young couple decided they would marry. The nineteen-year-old groom to be and his bride to be were traveling on horseback to the home of the minister who was to perform the wedding. As they rode along, no doubt making plans and contemplating their future together, clouds filled the sky and a fierce storm arose suddenly. As they sought shelter beneath a tree, lightning stuck another tree causing it to fall toward them. The tree hit the young couple. Mary was killed instantly. Tom was struck but survived the horrific ordeal, though his injuries would remain with him for the rest of his life. His arm was crippled and was practically useless to him from that time on. His wrist was also broken and remained crooked. Both horses were killed as well.

T. M. Allen

A day of great happiness was instantly turned to a day of great sorrow. For Tom, his plan for life and love was taken from him in a matter of minutes. How quickly one's life can change. The pain of a grief-stricken heart outweighed the pain of Tom's broken body. When Tom returned home, his parents were surprised to see him returning not as a healthy and cheerful young husband but as a young man permanently injured and alone.

This young man was Thomas Miller Allen, better known in restoration history as T. M. Allen. He would become one of the great preachers who played a vital role among Christians in the nineteenth century, especially in the states of Kentucky and Missouri.

T. M. Allen was born in the Shenandoah Valley of Virginia on the banks of the Shenandoah River on October 21, 1797. His parents were good people of the Presbyterian faith. When T. M. was sixteen years old, he entered the Virginia regiment as a non-commissioned officer to serve in the War of 1812, which ended about six months after his enlistment, and he was discharged at the termination of the conflict.

A few years after this, interested in travel, T. M. made his way to Kentucky. There he met Mary Van Meter, who became the love of his life and the one with whom he thought he would spend all his life. On May 10, 1816, the horrible turn of events took Mary's life and crippled T. M.

T. M. returned to Shenandoah County, Virginia to study law, but he soon moved to Fayette County, Kentucky. Not long after his arrival, he married Miss Rebecca Williamson Russell. Barton W. Stone performed the ceremony on March 24, 1818. The couple settled on a little farm near Lexington, Kentucky.

After his marriage, Allen continued his study of law at Transylvania. But in the spring of 1822 he moved to Bloomington, Indiana with one of his fellow law graduates, James Whitcomb. Whitcomb later became Governor of Indiana and a U. S. Senator from Indiana from 1849 until his death in 1852. Allen was very successful in the practice of law but returned to his farm in Kentucky in 1823.

Allen had begun to search for the answers to religious questions that were bothering him and was described as having an "uneasy conscience." He felt a keen responsibility to preach the message he had learned from Barton W. Stone. He soon closed his law office and prepared to enter the ministry of the Word of Christ. On June 23 of that year, Stone planted a church at "Old Union" in Fayette County.

Allen and his wife were among the first six original members of this church.

It was during this time, T. M. Allen began reading Alexander Campbell's paper, *The Christian Baptist*. As he became influenced by the things he read in the periodical, the more he could see the need to return to New Testament Christianity. When Jacob Creath, Sr., and Jacob Creath, Jr. were excluded from the Baptist Association in 1830 for their position in opposition to all human creeds, Allen became more convinced of returning to the Bible as the only creed. This fueled his labors in evangelism in Kentucky, resulting in the establishment of churches at Paris, Clintonville, and Bryant Station.

In 1836, T. M. Allen left Fayette County, Kentucky, for Boone County, Missouri. He located on the "Two-Mile Prairie." At once, he began to preach and spend much of his time traveling and preaching the ancient gospel. He spoke in private houses, barns, outside in open groves, in courthouses, in nearly all the meetinghouses in that part of the state, and in the Hall of Representatives at Jefferson City, Missouri. His labors as an evangelist proved successful in that part of the country.

T. M. Allen had been influenced by the *The Christian Baptist*, and through his influence, Allen was able to get Alexander Campbell to visit Missouri and strengthen the churches. Allen's association with Campbell continued as Allen frequently sent in reports to Campbell's new publication, *Millennial Harbinger*.

T. M. Allen has been described by George L. Peters, in an unpublished address on Allen, as "a model evangelist and pioneer preacher, having talents of a high order, a liberal education, refined manners, and a commanding appearance, with the gospel at the end of his tongue." He is also described as a "highly sympathetic speaker," capable of moving his audiences. The response to Allen's preaching bears witness to his ability to preach. It is said that thousands turned to the truth through his preaching. Crowds would follow him from one preaching appointment to another, just to hear him.

In Alvin Jennings book, T. M. Allen, Pioneer Preacher, Jennings wrote:

> Allen was a successful business man. He was what would be called a 'wealthy man.' He contributed liberally of his means to the endowment fund of Bethany College. His interest in that college grew out of his desire to see the churches supplied with an educated ministry. He was a friend of education and was one of the earliest and truest friends of Missouri University located at Columbia. He was honored a number of times by being elected president of the board of directors.

T. M. Allen continued to preach until death called him home on October 10, 1871. He died at Columbia, Missouri. Speaking at his funeral was Joseph K. Rogers, President of Missouri University. It is said that his funeral was attended by one of the largest crowds ever seen in Columbia, Missouri. Doors of businesses were closed during the funeral. The large crowd attending the funeral was a testimony to the love and appreciation so many had for him. T. M. Allen was a man who humbly walked with God.

The young man, spared from death on his wedding day fifty-five years earlier, had a profound effect on the lives of thousands as a gospel preacher.

Chapter 21

Alexander Campbell's Family Connection to Alabama

"Alexander Campbell preached here" is about as common among members of churches of Christ as "George Washington slept here" on the signs of inns from Virginia to New York. Over the years, I have heard brethren in North Alabama exclaim that Campbell preached in their community. The truth is that Campbell never made a trip through North Alabama and the closest he came to North Alabama was Tuscaloosa to the south and Nashville to the north. Campbell kept meticulous records, wrote of his travels, and published them in the *Millennial Harbinger*. If he ever traveled through North Alabama, he failed to mention it. F. B. Srygley tells an interesting story about three gospel preachers from North Alabama who rode on horseback sixty or seventy miles to hear Campbell speak in Tuscaloosa.

> Old Brother (John) Taylor and the two older Randolph's (Jerry and Lorenzo Dow) rode on horseback from that part of the state (Fayette County) to hear Campbell preach. Campbell preached for two hours on the change of the law. The three men left immediately after the meeting for their homes in Fayette County. Soon after leaving, one of the Randolph's said: 'After hearing that man preach, I do not feel that I could ever preach again.' The other one said: 'After hearing him preach, I do not feel that I ever have really preached' (*Gospel Advocate*, Sept. 3, 1936).

With this said, it is interesting to note that Alexander Campbell had members of his immediate family living in

North Alabama, in Lawrence County, having moved there after Campbell's death. His two daughters, Decima, (with her husband, Dr. John Judson Barclay) and Emma (with her husband Dr. Robert G. Barclay), and several grandchildren lived on the Ingleside Plantation in Lawrence County, Alabama, across the road and just north of General Joseph Wheeler's plantation, "Pond Spring." Emma was Campbell's adopted daughter and niece of Alexander's wife, Selina. (Emma was raised in the Campbell's home at Bethany, West Virginia.) Selina Campbell lived at Ingleside Plantation for awhile after Alexander Campbell's death and worked on her book, <u>Home Life and Reminiscences of Alexander Campbell</u>, which was published in 1882.

The Barclay boys were the sons of Dr. James Turner Barclay and his wife, Julia. The Barclays were a prominent Virginia family, having bought Thomas Jefferson's mansion, Monticello. The Barclay boys were born at Monticello. James T. Barclay was the first missionary of the American Christian Missionary Society, formed in 1849. He was sent to Jerusalem, where he accomplished little other than finding "Barclay's Gate," an original gate entrance to the Jewish Temple, and writing a book titled <u>The City of the Great King</u>. He returned to America in 1855.

After Dr. James Barclay returned to America, President Franklin Pierce placed him in charge of the Philadelphia mint to conduct experiments to prevent counterfeiting and deterioration of the metallic currency. Barclay was successful in this attempt. When the matter of remuneration for his discovery was brought before Congress, a bill passed the House giving him $100,000.00. It failed to pass the Senate by one vote. In 1858, James Barclay returned to the missionary work in Jerusalem, but when the Civil War broke out in 1861, he resigned his position and returned to the United States. In 1868, he moved to North Alabama, where he spent the remainder of his life. He organized the church in Wheeler, Alabama, near Ingleside Plantation and spoke in other settings as opportunities came (John T. Brown,

Churches of Christ, 1904 edition). One of his lectures was given at Florence, Alabama, in the Court House. The *Moulton Advertiser*, May 21, 1869, reported:

> Elder Barclay—This Reverend gentlemen (sic), as will be seen from the notice elsewhere in our columns, will preach in the Court House here, on Friday night, the eleventh of June next. Mr. Barclay has been for many years a Missionary in Palestine, and we may all expect to have a rich treat from his discourse.—*Florence Journal*

Dr. James T. Barclay died in North Alabama and was buried in the Ingleside Plantation cemetery. Confusion over where James T. Barclay was buried has been a controversy for many years among restoration historians. John T. Brown's Churches of Christ, printed in 1904, gives a biographical sketch of James T. Barclay, which was written by his grandson, J. T. (Jim) Barclay. Jim stated that his grandfather Barclay was buried in Alabama. However, there is no stone for him in the Ingleside Cemetery in Alabama, and there is a beautiful stone in the Campbell cemetery in Bethany, West Virginia bearing his name and the name of his wife, Julia Ann Barclay.

The answer to this mystery is that Dr. James Barclay was buried in Alabama and his body exhumed in 1906 (two years after John T. Brown's account) and was moved to Bethany. According to the *Moulton Advertiser* newspaper (May 18, 1906), Decima Campbell Barclay's husband, Dr. J. Judson Barclay, exhumed his father's body in 1906, and carried it back to Bethany, West Virginia, to be buried in the Campbell family cemetery, God's Acre, a short distance from the Bethany mansion.

The newspaper account is as follows:

> Decatur, Ala., May 12.—Dr. J. J. Barckley, (sic) of Virginia, who has been here on a visit, has just had the body of his father exhumed. His father was buried near

Hillsboro in the year 1874, where it has remained ever since. The body was buried in a metallic casket, and when exhumed, the body, and even the clothing was in a perfect state of preservation. For many years Dr. Barckley (sic) lived near Wheeler station, on the Southern railroad, sixteen miles west of Decatur. He married a daughter of the Rev. Alexander Campbell, the founder of the Campbellite church. Dr. Barckley (sic) is himself a minister.

The Campbells and Barclays were close through the marriage of their children, but Julia Barclay and Selina Campbell were closest friends and confidants and had been for years. Not only had their children married each other, Selina and Julia were alike in many ways. Both of their husbands were preachers, and Selina and Julia shared their innermost thoughts through a number of letters. This union was made closer when Dr. James T. Barclay and his wife, Julia, moved to Lawrence County, Alabama after the Civil War and Dr. Barclay preached at the church near the plantation. Selina Campbell shared much of her time between her daughters, Virginia in Kentucky, and Decima and Emma in Alabama, and she was able to see her old friend, Julia Barclay, on a regular basis. The church near Ingleside Plantation was known as Ingleside Chapel. Dr. James T. Barclay (who had been one of the most prominent men in the brotherhood) preached for the little church. Selina Campbell gave money for the erecting of the chapel, and when dedicated, T. B. Larimore, David Walk, and J. M. Pickens spoke at the dedication of the chapel (*World Evangelist*, June 1987).

There were at least two reasons why Mrs. Alexander Campbell returned to Alabama again and again. First, Selina was comforted in the faithfulness of her daughters and their families. Selina was disappointed in the lack of spirituality in some of Alexander's offspring. But Decima and Emma were strong in the faith and had married strong Christian men. Selina's son-in-law, Judson Barclay (Decima's husband), was a gospel preacher and a writer for one of the brotherhood papers, *Southern Christian Weekly*, published at Mountain Home, Alabama (only a few miles from Ingleside) from 1872-1879. In his secular work, he was the president and a director of Kaolin and Mineral Company of Decatur, Alabama (Barclay box, Lawrence County Archives), and is mentioned in several places as Dr. J. J. Barclay. (His brother, Robert G. Barclay, is listed in the 1870 Lawrence County, Alabama census, as a physician.)

Second, Selina Campbell was especially close to her granddaughter, Virginia Huntington Barclay, Decima's daughter. Virginia (Virgie) was born in Cyprus in 1864, while her father, John Judson Barclay, was with the U. S. Consul in Cyprus. When the Barclays returned to the United States, Virgie was a toddler. The child was a sickly one, having experienced several physical problems, including an accidental poisoning. Selina Campbell held a great fondness for Virgie, and she enjoyed spending time with her young granddaughter.

Virgie had to wear a steel brace on her neck and a tightening jacket with a chin cup that was painful to wear, and those around her suffered to watch her. Dr. Loretta Long in her book, Selina Campbell, A Fellow Solider of the Cross, wrote: "The family letters say more about Selina's relationship with Virgie than about any relationship Selina sustained with her other grandchildren." Long goes on to say "the girl was the light of the home in which she lived. Even though often bedridden, she still sang hymns and remained cheerful and happy."

In spite of Virgie's physical difficulties, she grew into a beautiful young woman. However, in June 1882, the favorite grandchild of Selina Campbell died when she fell victim to what was termed "a congestion of the brain." (Today this condition is called encephalitis.) She was eighteen years old.

The *Moulton Advertiser* ran two obituaries of Virgie Barclay in its Thursday, September 28, 1882 edition. One was from the Wheeling, West Virginia *Daily Intelligencer* account, dated September 16, 1882, and the other was the local newspaper account. The following is the *Daily Intelligencer* account of Virgie's death:

> Wheeling, West Virginia Daily Intelligencer, September 16, 1882—The many friends and acquaintances in this city of Miss Virgie Barclay, of Alabama, who has been spending the summer at the home of her uncle, Col. Aleck Campbell, at Bethany, were greatly shocked yesterday to learn of her death. This sad event occurred about 10 o'clock the night before, after an illness of ten days, which finally resulted in congestion of the brain. The fate of this accomplished and lovely lady, who had just turned her eighteenth year, is inexpressibly sad. She was the only daughter of her parents, Mr. and Mrs. J. J. Barclay, of Lawrence county (sic), Alabama, and she had been born to them and partially reared in a foreign land, when Mr. Barclay was the United States Consul at the island of Cyprus, in the Mediterranean. She had grown up and been educated amidst all the endearments and refinements of her home in the South, and seemed more like a younger sister than a daughter to her devoted parents. They had lavished on her a world of affection, and her accomplished mother seemed to literally live in the light of her eyes. Scarcely a wish of her life had been left ungratified, and her hopes and prospects for the future seemed as fair and enchanting as any that earth could offer. "None knew her but to love her, nor named her but to praise." And yet the grim monster whose arrow always seeks a "shining mark" leveled suddenly at this dear and sweet spirited girl, the dart that laid her low, and all the hearts of near and dear relatives are crushed by the inscrutable blow. Her funeral will take place this afternoon at 2 o'clock, from the home of Col. Aleck Campbell, and the remains be interred in the family burying grounds adjoining the old

mansion of her grandfather, the lamented Alexander Campbell.

In June 1868, Tolbert Fanning traveled from Nashville on a tour into Alabama and Mississippi. He traveled from Nashville to Athens and on to Decatur. From Decatur, the train heading west passed by the Ingleside Plantation. Dr. James Wilburn, in his biography of Fanning, The Hazard of the Die, stated: "He passed the farm of J. T. Barclay, son-in-law of Alexander Campbell and the first man sent out by the American Christian Missionary Society, who had returned from his work in Jerusalem." This statement is obviously wrong on two accounts and needs to be corrected. J. T. Barclay did not own the farm, and he was not the son-in-law of Alexander Campbell. He was the father of two of Campbell's sons-in-law.

Selina Campbell stayed very busy after the death of her husband, Alexander. She was a prolific writer and loved to read. In a letter to T. B. Larimore, headed Ingleside Plantation near Wheeler's Station, December 14, 1874, Mrs. Campbell applauded Larimore's forthcoming journal, *Angel of Mercy, Love, Peace, and Truth*. (Volume 1, number 1 was dated January 1875.) Mrs. Campbell was highly pleased with the journal. From the letter, we find that Larimore had asked Mrs. Campbell to write for the journal, but she refused, stating the need to leave for Louisville, Kentucky, to visit her daughter there, and she said that she "was under a great trial, in seeing a lovely little daughter greatly afflicted." Mrs. Campbell went on to write:

> Under the circumstances, I requested J. J. Barclay, to write for me, and say to you, 'that it would indeed afford me the greatest pleasure to assist, if it were in the smallest way, in the moulding (sic) of the thought or in the training of the young'. But such were my engagements that I feared and hesitated to promise.

The circumstances of her "greatly afflicted" daughter in Kentucky were the marital and financial difficulties of her daughter, Virginia Thompson. Virginia's husband, William Thompson, an attorney, had developed a drinking problem that affected his ability to earn a living for his family and had piled up debts that could not be paid. Selina was troubled about Virginia's situation. Virginia was on the verge of losing everything and was facing a public auction to liquidate her household possessions to satisfy the debts to her creditors. Mrs. Campbell was able to help Virginia in securing some personal items, but at this time Mrs. Campbell was also experiencing financial difficulty (Long, pp. 162-163).

When Alexander Campbell died, his farm was one of the most successful farms in Virginia, and he was a wealthy man. However, the estate was divided among several children, and the farm soon declined, probably from lack of proper management. The money simply ran out. Mrs. Campbell concluded the letter to T. B. Larimore by saying in a postscript, "I enclose $5.00 as a small token of my desire for its success. I could wish it was (sic) Ten Fold as Much as it is. I do hope you will succeed in raising much to aid you in the paper and the building."

The financial woes of Selina Campbell continued. In 1876, her son William decided to sell the Campbell mansion, claiming that his mother had signed the house over to him as collateral on a loan he needed, and therefore the mansion was on the note. Decima tried to purchase the mansion for her mother but was unable to do so. The mansion was sold and no longer belonged to the Campbell family. However, three years later in 1879, Decima was able to regain possession of the property from a subsequent owner, and Selina Campbell moved back into the mansion (Long, pp. 156-157).

Eventually, Judson and Decima moved back to Bethany to the Campbell mansion. Judson Barclay, who had experience in the diplomatic corps, having served as Vice-

Consul to Beirut, Syria in 1858, and as consul in Cyprus from 1859-1865), was appointed Consul General to Tangier, Morocco from 1893-1896. Decima, who appeared to be the "pack rat" of the family, preserved a number of her father's private documents. Among these documents was Alexander Campbell's diary, which Campbell had titled *"Journal of a Voyage from Ireland Towards America, 1808."* These documents and the journal were discovered in 1964 in Australia and were given to the Disciples of Christ Historical Society, located in Nashville, Tennessee.

How did the documents end up in Australia? Decima's son, Julian T. Barclay, had married a girl named Mary, who was born in Australia. Julian and Mary decided to immigrate to Australia. Decima died on the eve of Julian and Mary's departure for Adelaide, Australia. Julian and Mary's three children, Julian, Audine and John, traveled with them. Julian and Mary lived in Australia from 1920 to 1929 and from 1935 to 1938. The family then returned to the United States. Julian died in 1948 and is buried in the Campbell Family Cemetery Plot #30. Sixteen years after his death, an old trunk was found which contained the lost documents, including valuable manuscripts and scores of sermons preached by Alexander Campbell when he was in his early twenties. Julian's daughter, Audine Andrews, found the old trunk in 1960. Not knowing the value of the contents, the trunk was stored in a shed until 1964. While cleaning out the shed in 1964, Audine was faced with the problem of what she could do with these family documents. Eventually, they were reported to someone associated with the Australian churches of Christ. The finding of these documents and their contents was reported to the State Executive Committee, and on Friday, June 19, 1964, Audine Barclay Andrews' cousin, Mrs. E. V. Lawton, delivered these documents to the State Executive Committee of the Australian churches of Christ in a soap powder box. They decided to have them microfilmed and then sent to the Disciples of Christ Historical Society, in

Nashville, Tennessee. This treasure trove of Campbell materials has now been preserved.

On a trip to the Disciples of Christ Historical Society a few years ago, this writer had chill bumps as he gazed upon and held Campbell's personal diary that was found 156 years after Campbell began writing it. This diary had endured the shipwreck of the Hibernia in 1808, and was one of the items Campbell was able to save from the sinking ship. The diary had taken an amazing journey from Ireland to America, America to Australia, and from Australia back to America.

Julian T. Barclay's wife, Mary, must have been married to Julian while in Lawrence County, Alabama. Several letters from Miss Annie Wheeler (daughter of CSA and US General Joseph Wheeler) were written to Mary from 1942 to 1945 and show that a great friendship existed between the two women. The Wheeler plantation was very close to the Barclay plantation. It is evident that Julian and Mary were back in the United States at that time and that Mary had inquired about moving to Florence, Alabama. (Julian and Mary had returned from Australia in 1938.) In one of the letters, Annie Wheeler responded to a letter from Mary about Jim Barclay (son of Emma and Robert G. Barclay), who was still living on the plantation. Annie wrote:

> I rarely see him. He is still living the same way at old home. He begun many years ago studying our Bible, and then joined so many Bible Societies in different parts of the world - being a hermit - I am told that he has never left the place (Ingleside Plantation) since the day in 1917 that he went to Hillsboro and saw the boys leave for France.

Jim Barclay may have been a hermit, but his personal ledger, dated 1942, shows a competent and astute business manager, detailing expenditures for the plantation.

Robert G. and Emma Barclay stayed in Alabama. Robert Barclay died in 1876, and Emma lived another fifty-two years and died at the age of eighty-six in 1928. Both are buried in the Ingleside Plantation cemetery in Lawrence County, Alabama.

When Robert G. Barclay's estate was probated in 1877, it was reported that his personal estate consisted of 685 acres of land and that his widow, Emma C. Barclay, and four minor children, Julia Barclay, Louisa Barclay, James (Jim) Barclay, and Selina Barclay, survived him. Their son, Jim Barclay, remained at Ingleside through 1944. On December 28, 1944, Probate Judge Isaac Johnson, Jr. heard a petition against Jim Barclay, then seventy-seven years old. The petition was designated a "lunacy inquisition." Jim Barclay was found to be "non compos mentis," described in the petition as having a weak mind and not able to look after the estate. He was confined to the "Bryce Hospital in Tuscaloosa, Alabama, an institution for the feeble minded." Jim Barclay would not remain in Bryce Hospital for long. He died on July 2, 1945, six months after being sent to the mental hospital. (Court Documents)

In one of Miss Annie Wheeler's letters to Mary Barclay, she told of Jim Barclay being removed from Ingleside. She wrote:

> When the papers were all fixed up, he (Barclay Phinizy, Jim's nephew) got the Sheriff and others went to him - they having arranged previously with one of the colored men to remove the pistol, without his notice. Barclay went in first and asked him if he would go to Texas and live with him, he said most 'emphaticaly (sic) "'NO'". Then the sheriff went in and spoke in a calm and kind but strong and firm voice, telling him it was out of the question for him to stay there and the decision was made to move him to a comfortable place, where he would be under the care of specialist and capable nurses, and he made no further objection...He had to be taken up and dressed just like a baby, but made an easy and successful trip (Annie Wheeler, letter to Mary

Barclay, December 30, 1944, Barclay box, Moulton, Alabama Archives).

After the death of Jim Barclay, court documents showed a confusion of heirs and legal claims. Some of the plantation had been sold to the Tennessee Valley Authority. After Jim Barclay's death, the plantation ceased to exist, and the home has been torn down. Thus ends an interesting story of the Alexander Campbell family connection to North Alabama.

Chapter 22

John Henry: The Walking Bible

The story of John Henry, the steel driving man, is the stuff of legends. As with most legends, they are usually based on some truth. "John Henry, the steel driving man," was a former slave, born in Holly Springs, Mississippi, and became famous when he won a race with a new contraption called the steam powered steel driver. Witnesses stated that John Henry beat the steam drill in a contest that took place on Oak Mountain near Birmingham, Alabama in 1887. John Henry died almost immediately after the contest when he collapsed and his wife was called to his side. He died in her arms. The measurement showed that the steam drill had drilled 21 feet and John Henry 27 ½ feet.

While many have heard of John Henry, the steel driving man, few are aware of another John Henry. This John Henry was a gospel preacher. He was a man of great physical presence and even greater mental capacity. The story of this John Henry is worthy of legendary status, though few even know his name. This John Henry never desired fame but evidently felt as the apostle Paul described when he stated in 1 Corinthians 9:16, "For though I preach the gospel, I have nothing to glory of: for necessity is laid upon me; yea, woe is unto me, if I preach not the gospel!" Henry felt that he must also preach the gospel to the best of his ability to a lost and dying generation in desperate need of preachers.

John Henry was born in Washington County, Pennsylvania, on October 1, 1797. His religious background was Presbyterian. He was converted in 1828 under the teaching of Adamson Bentley at a schoolhouse in Austintown, Ohio, where William Hayden was the schoolmaster. (William Hayden would later become one of the great gospel preachers of the restoration movement.) At the conclusion of Bentley's first discourse, Henry presented himself for baptism. His wife was baptized at the same time. Henry would become a powerful force of the restoration movement in the Western Reserve, known today as Ohio.

John Henry was a plain man. It was noted that he always wore the plainest of clothing, and he was just as plain in his preaching. He was described as an untiring laborer, quick to decide, and prompt to act.

A. S. Hayden, in his book History of the Disciples on the Western Reserve, said that John Henry was:

> [T]all, rather spare, with sandy complexion and sharp features, quick in movement, as in the operations of his mind, and when he walked he planted his feet with a tread which showed the firmness of the man. Cheerful at times almost to levity, very social, kind hearted, and with a wit like a polished rapier, whatever 'his hand found to do he did with his might' (Hayden, p. 134).

Hayden also wrote:

> Though uncultured, he was not rude. He was high-minded and honorable, and immensely popular with the people. On one occasion John Henry and Alexander Campbell met near Minerva, Ohio, where both were scheduled to speak. Most of the people did not know Henry from Campbell, and as Campbell finished his oration, many of the hearers said, 'We wish that man would sit down, and let Campbell get up, for he knows how to preach' (Hayden, p. 135)!

Though not trained in oratory, Henry was considered a great orator, even greater than Alexander Campbell in the estimation of many. Hayden said that "as a speaker, few equaled him in instructive and entertaining discourse. But the power of his sermons was much in the authority with which they were spoken, and that he often moved on great assemblies with a mastery that chained attention for two hours" (Hayden, p. 134).

William Baxter, in his biography, Life of Walter Scott, gave this description of John Henry. He "was tall, spare of flesh, and angular." John Henry began to speak publicly somewhat by accident. Baxter continued his description of Henry, writing:

> On one occasion when some rude fellows made a disturbance at a baptism when he was present, and he felt impelled to reprove them, which he did with such force and vigor, that many who were present discovered in him the elements of a successful public speaker; the result was, that he was called upon to speak at the meetings of the church, and in a short time his success exceeded the most sanguine hopes of his friends. He did not seem to have thought himself possessed of any such ability; but as soon as it became evident, he lost no opportunity of usefulness. He supported himself by the labor of his hands; and when his labors were demanded in the gospel field, he only required that a man should be put in his place to do the customary work on the farm, and he, in the meantime, would labor quite as faithfully in the pulpit and from house to house.
>
> He was at the time of his conversion a plain, industrious farmer; distinguished, however, by a ready natural wit and a musical talent, which was truly wonderful. On wind and stringed instruments, he was a ready player, and sang with fine taste and feeling; and even composed music with ease. When the Bible was substituted for creed and catechism, he eagerly devoted himself to its study, and with such success that few men ever became more familiar with its language. His knowledge of it was so full and accurate that he was said to have committed the whole inspired volume to memory, and was commonly spoken of as the Bible with a tongue in it, or the Walking Bible; one thing, however, is certain, he could quote, without the least hesitancy or mistake, all

the passages upon any given subject, at the same time giving chapter and verse, and could recite at will chapters from the Old or New Testament, from the Gospels, Epistles, Prophets, or Psalms, with the greatest facility; and, in addition to this, he seemed to have a clear conception of the scope and meaning of the whole. He was quick at repartee, and the object of it had never to weary himself to find the point of the retort— that was always felt.

Dwight Stevenson, in his book, <u>Voice of the Golden Oracle</u>, wrote:

> He (Henry) also had an elephantine memory. Reputedly, he memorized the whole Bible. He was later known far and wide as the 'Bible with a Tongue in It,' or the 'Walking Bible.' It was said that he could quote all passages on any subject with chapter and verse. His preaching, delivered in rapid syllables as fast as the ear could catch them, was nearly all in scriptural language. Mixing preaching with farming at the beginning, farming soon became the avocation, and was then crowded out entirely, as this earnest man followed a pattern which was to become common on the Western Reserve.

Henry K. Shaw, in his book, <u>Buckeye Disciples</u>, wrote:

> Henry had a "great power of oratory" and that his speech was "exceeding rapid." The power of his speech was the "clearness with which he set forth his views and the deep and unaffected earnestness of his manners." Henry understood the various religious systems of the day, and in his exposure of departures from the Word of God and the substitution of human inventions, he often reminded his hearers of the prophets who reproved the Israelites for their departures from the law of their God. Henry came to be in such demand as a preacher that he had to give up his farm life and devote himself to sowing the

good seed of the Kingdom, which he did so successfully that many in whose hearts the good seed fell, to this day thank God for his faithful and earnest labors.

One of the earliest references to John Henry in the literature is a letter sent to Walter Scott and published in *The Evangelist* in 1832. Scott said he received a letter from brother William Hayden on the Western Reserve "where he, brother John Henry, and three others, are laboring. We are informed one hundred and thirty have been immersed within a few months" (*The Evangelist*, 1832, p. 24). On September 17, 1836, A. S. Hayden wrote the *Millennial Harbinger* saying, "Brother Henry assisted us in a two day's meeting in Deerfield, ending last Lord's Day. The disciples were much enlivened, and six joyful and intelligent persons submitted to the Saviour" (*MH*, 1836, p. 478). On February 13, 1839, W. O'Connor wrote from Euclid, Ohio, of a gospel meeting in which brother Henry preached and reported 10 baptisms. He said, "May the Lord bless the labors of brother John Henry, that he may turn many to righteousness and receive a crown of rejoicing in the kingdom of Jesus! And God shall have the praise through Jesus Christ" (*MH*, 1840, p. 184).

A letter to the *Millennial Harbinger* dated December 5, 1839, sent by John Henry to Alexander Campbell, stated:

> I take this opportunity to inform you that I set out in the month of October last, to hold a few meetings with the brethren in this part of the world, and had the misfortune to have my ankle bone put out of place the very first day. Our first meeting was in Fairfield, Columbiana county (sic)...Nineteen obeyed the gospel...The second meeting was in Sharon, and ten obeyed. The third was in Hartford, where six obeyed. The fourth was in Southington, where eleven obeyed and two received on confession, and five were added to our congregation since the third Lord's day in October. So from the

above date I have seen fifty three confess the Lord (*Millennial Harbinger*, 1840, p. 41).

By 1841, John Henry's ability as a preacher had developed to the point that he participated in a number of debates. John Henry claimed he had engaged in four debates recently on the subject of baptism, "and no one hurt" (*MH*, 1841, pp. 331-332).

One of these debates took place in the autumn of 1841. Some of the Methodist preachers had taken a vow to root out the so called "heresy" since they determined the teaching of the Disciples in the Western Reserve to be false. The most important of these encounters took place at Newton Falls in the autumn of 1841.

A Mr. Waldo was selected to destroy the Disciples. He was a well educated man, a classical scholar and a man of learning. No doubt, he felt like Goliath facing David as the battle of words began. John Henry had been chosen by the Disciples to champion and defend the word of God. Henry's vast knowledge of the Bible and ability to quote the Book proved to be a wise choice on their part. Baxter wrote:

> His thoughts were well defined, and uttered with a rapidity which required the closest attention to keep up with them; so self-possessed that it was impossible to throw him off his guard; perfectly original in his treatment of his subject; without an equal in that region in a knowledge of the Scriptures, which he quoted from memory as readily and accurately as others could read from the open book; quick and keen in repartee, and able to preserve his gravity while giving utterance to things that convulsed his audience with laughter, and yet so deeply and solemnly in earnest as to often make his hearers feel as if the judgment day were at hand.

William Baxter tells the following account of this debate:

When Mr. Waldo arose to speak, he could neither conceal his confidence in his own abilities and advantages, nor his contempt for the views he was to assail and the foe over which he expected to gain an easy victory. Indeed, he did not regard the subject as one requiring serious argument; the views of the Disciples were only fit themes for ridicule, and to the use of this weapon he applied himself in a strain somewhat as follows: The Campbellites have never understood the religion of Christ; they have never got into its heart; they are foolishly pecking away at the outside; they are sticking in the bark; they are like the old fiddler who was standing on a bridge looking at the stream flow by; his fiddle fell from its case into the river, and, as it floated away, one of the bystanders said, 'Your fiddle is gone.' 'Never mind,' said the fiddler, 'all is right; I have got the case all safe,' and he hugged the box that had contained the instrument closer than ever before. He then proceeded: 'I give the Campbellites warning, that they may expect rough handling. I was accustomed as well as my opponent to swing the axe and the maul when I was young. I know how to give hard blows; let them look out. The Campbellites are like a parrot, ever repeating the same thing, always crying out 'water! water!' It is water that purifies the heart! These poor creatures do not understand the Bible.

He for some other reason compared the Campbellites, as he called them, to a pair of sheep-shears, and with such material made himself merry, wholly unconscious of the reckoning so near at hand; and, having fully exhausted his quiver of every shaft of wit and satire, with an air of perfect complacency and self-satisfaction, he took his seat.

John Henry's usually impassive features underwent frequent changes during this singular speech, and when he arose to reply, there was a dangerous light in his keen, piercing eyes. He was perfectly cool and collected, but it was the calm which precedes the blinding flash and the terrible thunder peal, and soon the bolt fell. He began by saying: 'My brethren have appointed me as a true yoke-fellow with Mr. Waldo, and I intend to follow him jump for jump; he has told of his great learning, his long study, his knowledge of the Bible, and every thing connected with it; while we, listening to his threats and boasts, sat in wonder and amazement at the mighty things that we were to hear and see today. But alas! alas! How we have been disappointed! The sum and substance of his speech, the entire fat and marrow of it, the product of his great learning and preparation, absolutely all the points he brought forth for me to answer are these, which I have noted down on this bit of paper— namely: 'hickory bark,' 'an empty fiddle-case,' 'a parrot,' and 'a pair of sheep shears;' these are the potent arguments to which he expects me to reply'— and, holding up his left hand, he enumerated them upon his fingers: 'First, hickory bark; second, an empty fiddle-case; third, a parrot; fourth, a pair of sheep shears'— and upon these he rung the charges, and made the task of answering them seem so hopeless, and at the same time so ludicrous, that the audience was convulsed with mirth and his opponent overwhelmed with shame and mortification. But the end was not yet. He proceeded: 'My friend Mr. Waldo has informed you that, though now a great scholar, he was once a laboring man; that in his youth he swung the axe and mallet. All I have to say on that point is, that his being here today alive and well is a certain proof that he knew better how to use those tools than he does how to use the Bible; for if he had handled the axe and mallet as awkwardly as he does the Bible, it's a God's blessing that he did not beat his brains out long years ago.

He then assailed, in the most merciless manner, Mr. Waldo's method of quoting Scripture. 'My friend,' said he, 'has given us but little proof of his biblical knowledge; the little he did quote— 'Faith that works by love purifies the heart'—was inaccurate;

he took two unconnected passages and stuck them together, and quoted that for Scripture. You can make any thing you please out of the Bible in that way. Let me try.' On the last great day of the feast, Jesus stood and cried, By the Gods of Pharaoh ye are all spies.' 'Thou shalt not muzzle the ox that treadeth out the corn, for of such is the kingdom of heaven.' 'Judas went out and hanged himself; go thou and do likewise, and what thou doest, do quickly.' There, that is the way Mr. Waldo quotes Scripture."

The effect of this speech, rapid and sharp as the discharge of musketry, was truly wonderful; the audience was convulsed with laughter, and the blow came so sudden and unexpected upon Mr. Waldo that he looked upon Henry in blank astonishment; the smiling and self-satisfied look with which he had taken his seat but a short time before gave place to such a sudden and ridiculous sobriety as was ludicrous in the extreme, and the most serious man in the house could not restrain himself at beholding his puzzled, amazed, and confounded look. This terrible onslaught Henry followed by a clear and convincing presentation of the teaching of the Bible on the points at issue, which was perfectly overwhelming.

Over the years, reports of John Henry's work continued to flow to the *Millennial Harbinger*. Most of the reports were by others appreciative of Henry's work. A report, dated January 1843 from the Bedford church, stated they held a successful meeting with J. H. Jones and John Henry preaching. Dr. J. P. Robison reported, "The last three weeks in Cuyahoga County, some two hundred have yielded in obedience to the faith of the prophets and apostles (*Millennial Harbinger*, 1843, p. 46). J. P. Robison reported from Bedford, Ohio, in a letter dated January 19, 1843, 'We have just closed a meeting in our place in which we were assisted by brothers J H. Jones and J. Henry. Eighty-four penitent believers were baptized' (*Millennial Harbinger*, 1843, p. 142). The same year, a report stated, 'Brother J. H. Jones and

A. B. Green (went) to Aurora, with brother John Henry, and immersed 38 persons' (*Millennial Harbinger*, 1842, p. 334).

By 1842, John Henry had reached his stride as a gospel preacher. He was constantly in demand, and his demanding schedule required him to move about to different locations. Several reports tell us of the desire of the brethren to have John Henry remain with them so that the sheaves could be gathered in their community. Benjamin Pritchard said, "If they (Henry and Lanphear) could have continued eight or ten days, there would have been a great deal done (*Millennial Harbinger* 1840, p. 280). J. Turner wrote of Henry and said, if only "could he have tarried a few days longer, I think many more would have obeyed the gospel" (*Millennial Harbinger*, 1842, p. 90). J. G. Nikerson wrote, "Could brother Henry remain a few days longer, I think many more would obey the gospel. All that is wanting here to insure success, is a proper teacher" (*Millennial Harbinger*, 1940, p. 189).

Two months before John Henry's death, a brother R. Downing wrote to Barton Stone's paper, the *Christian Messenger*, telling of the work of John Henry and others as they continued to convert disciples from the Methodist churches, which assured these men of being the recipients of wrath of preachers for these groups. Downing wrote:

> Through the labors of John Henry, J. J. Moss, James E. Gaston and others, we have lately had about one hundred additions to the good cause at four or five different points near this place, and we are much indebted to our Methodist friends for their quota of the above number, for the Truth has drawn upon their ranks very liberally in so much that we hereby acknowledge the receipt of some thirty or forty Lambs from their Episcopal Fold, which has caused no little dissatisfaction among the Shepherds of this Methodist Israel. However we have the 'Vantage ground' for we have not as yet heard of their obtaining a single addition from the Christian

ranks, neither have they sprinkled any of our Babes and Children (*Christian Messenger*, February 1844, p. 319).

As with most preachers of his time, Henry felt that the brethren neglected to support gospel preachers. In a letter to the editor of the *Millennial Harbinger* in 1841, Henry complained "of the poor remuneration received for his services. What he wrote was an indictment of the manner in which ministers were treated by the churches. He wrote:

> There is an evil under the sun of which even Solomon, I believe, has not spoken—namely, the brethren are always writing to us to come and preach for them, and they forget to pay the postage. Hence my letter tax costs me more every year than my clothing. Will the brethren reform, and not lay a burden on us that neither our fathers nor we are able to bear (Shaw, p. 31).

It is likely that John Henry's converts numbered in the thousands and perhaps additional thousands could be added if he continued to live. This was not to be. Henry died of typhus fever when he was only forty-seven years old.

The report of his death was sent to Alexander Campbell and he responded to the sad news by writing:

> From the above melancholy tidings it appears that a great man has fallen in our Israel. Brother John Henry, as a preacher of a particular order of preachers, had no equal—no superior. He was not only mighty in the scriptures as a preacher and teacher, but was also eminently exemplary in the social virtues of Christianity. His praise is in all the churches in the Western Reserve and circumjacent country. His age, I presume, was not more than 50. His labors in the cause of reformation were very considerable. The useful life and excellent character will long be remembered in many of his acquaintance

and brethren. We sincerely sympathize with his bereaved wife and afflicted family. Well for them that there is one of omnipotent power and whose 'mercy endureth forever.' Who has promised to be, among the saints, a husband to the widow and father to the fatherless (*Millennial Harbinger*, 1844, p. 288)!

A detailed obituary appeared later in the *Millennial Harbinger*. Written from Warren, Ohio, on May 13, 1844 by William Hayden and Cyrus Bosworth, reported:

> Dear brother Campbell—At the request of several of our teaching brethren present at the funeral, we communicate to you the intelligence of the death of our beloved brother in Christ, JOHN HENRY, who departed this life on the 1st instant.
>
> He was born October 1, 1797, of Presbyterian parents, who early instructed him in moral and religious sentiments. He embraced the principles of the gospel under the preaching of brother Bentley in 1828—soon became a most indefatigable and successful laborer in the 'the word'—a man of the most ardent temperament, warmth of affection, untiring zeal for the truth—a fearless and uncompromising advocate for the word of the Lord, which dwelt in him richly in much wisdom.
>
> A special messenger on the 12th of March reached him in Jefferson county (sic), with the intelligence of sickness in his family. He returned on the 13th, much fatigued from his journey and previous preaching in that region for several weeks, witnessed the recovery of his wife, and subsequently the death of his oldest son, a disciple of much promise—took sick, and anticipating his change, with triumphant resignation, while his senses remained, after some sixteen days confinement he died on the first of May. His funeral was numerously attended on the 2d. Discourse by brother Bracket from 1 Thess. 4:13-14 to a deeply afflicted audience.

In his death society had lost a pillar; the church, a chief man; the teaching brethren, a fellow-laborer. Few, if any, can fill the place to a wife and children, of a kind husband and affectionate parent. In commending them affectionately to the Father of the fatherless and the widow's God, we trust they will have the deepest sympathy of such as truly 'visit the widow and the fatherless in their affliction, and keep themselves unspotted from the world' (*Millennial Harbinger*, 1844, p. 335).

A. S. Hayden wrote:

> There was lamentation in all the churches when he died. The feeling is well remembered and distinctly defined. Brother John Henry, as a preacher of a particular order of preachers, had no equal—no superior. He was not only mighty in the Scriptures as preacher and teacher, but was also eminently exemplary in the social virtues of Christianity. His praise is in all the churches in the Western Reserve and circumjacent country (Hayden, p. 135).

In his fourteen years as a Christian, John Henry memorized the Bible and became recognized as one of the great preachers of his time. No doubt, there are multiplied thousands of Christians today who are descendants of those men and women converted to the truth under the teaching of "John Henry, The Walking Bible."

Chapter 23

T. B. Larimore—The Preacher

When Theophilus Brown Larimore departed this life at the age of eighty-five on March 18, 1929, at 9:30 A.M., the church of our Lord lost a great soldier. So honored and respected was he that the May 16th issue of *Gospel Advocate* could not contain all the accolades sent to the paper. And while his photograph graced the cover of the May 16th issue, the accolades would continue in the May 23rd issue of *Gospel Advocate*.

Larimore

Words of praise for the great gospel preacher poured forth from all parts of the country, extolling the kindness, simplicity, gentleness, love, and faith of the great man. Many articles graced the pages of *Gospel Advocate*, telling of the great talent of Larimore as a preacher, even comparing him to Alexander Campbell, Jesse B. Ferguson, and John T. Johnson. There is no doubt, had these things been said of brother Larimore in his presence, he would have blushed exceedingly. Larimore was a simple man, yet his sermons were the work of a wordsmith of great genius. Even today, when reading his sermons, the question comes forth, how could a simple man be so eloquent?

Born July 10, 1843, T. B. Larimore became a Christian after the Civil War. He served as a Confederate scout, and after being captured, he gave his oath of allegiance to the Federal Government, took his mother and sister, and moved from Sequatchie Valley, Tennessee, to Kentucky. In Hopkinsville, Kentucky, on his twenty-first birthday, July 10, 1864 Larimore obeyed the gospel. He began preaching almost immediately. He attended Franklin College in

Nashville and studied under Tolbert Fanning. In 1868, he came to Alabama as a school teacher in the Mountain Home School, operated by gospel preacher James Madison Pickens at Lawrence County. While drumming up students for Mountain Home School, Larimore found his way to the Rock Creek Church in what was then Franklin County, Alabama. On his way to Rock Creek, Larimore, so destitute he was thought to be a tramp, was accosted by some ruffians in Tuscumbia, Alabama, and with the help of a local barber, they shaved his head. This young, slender, tall, bald preacher made his way to Rock Creek to preach the gospel. His appearance was less than impressive.

From Rock Creek, he went to the Hopewell Church of Christ in Lauderdale County, about four miles north of Florence on the Jackson Military Road near the present day intersection of Cox Creek Parkway and Jackson Highway. The man, who was to become the greatest preacher in the brotherhood by the turn of the 20th century, was considered inadequate for the work at the Hopewell church. F. D. Srygley quotes Larimore in his book, <u>Larimore and His Boys</u>, saying:

> I came to Hopewell to hold a protracted meeting. They let me try to preach once, and they were so well pleased with that 'sarmint' that they let me off—suddenly! The meeting closed with a jerk and a bang. It was not wound up much, hence required but little time to run down; or, perhaps it ran down so very fast is why it struck down so quick. It was wound up for eight days and it ran down in an hour.

Larimore said that the brethren at Hopewell reasoned, "if we let him try to preach here, it is good bye to our prospects. Better have no preaching than his sort."

Since the brethren at Hopewell didn't want him preaching there, they were in a dilemma as to what to do with the young preacher. Finally, Brother Andrew Jackson Gresham (who would soon become Larimore's brother-in-law) loaded

Larimore in his buggy and carried him to another church some fourteen miles out in the country. They reasoned that "good preachers rarely go there; they will appreciate any kind of preaching." There was a group of "Hard Shell Baptists" meeting in that area of Lauderdale, County. Larimore went to this group and began a work that continues to this day. Originally known as the Bethel Bara church of Christ, southern slang reduced the name to Bethel Berry church of Christ.

The Mars Hill Years

On August 30, 1868, T. B. Larimore married Julia Esther Gresham. Esther had inherited twenty-eight acres of land, a part of the Gresham farm, from her father, Philemon Gresham. On that land, T. B. and Esther built their home. In 1871, the Larimore home became the centerpiece of what would become Mars Hill College. The college continued from 1871 to 1887. For seventeen years, the college would be a major chapter in the life of T. B. Larimore.

Beginning as Mars Hill Academy, the co-ed institution provided education for young men and women who would serve in leadership roles in the home, community, and the church in the twentieth century as the nineteenth century drew to a close. Larimore served as President of the College and taught classes daily. There was little time for rest as his days began early and lasted until late at night.

When Larimore began training boys to preach, he was only twenty-eight years old. He had much to learn about what he was teaching. F. D. Srygley said the boys at Mars Hill were taught:

> Earnestness was one of their chief elements of success in preaching. They believed all they preached, and preached all they believed. They preached it because they believed it, and preached it exactly as they believed it. No playing at preaching or mere

pulpit performances were encouraged at Mars' Hill. Sensational themes and studied formality in preaching were never mentioned but to be condemned.

In a letter to one of his boys on "how to preach," Larimore said:

> Fortunately, I have never been drilled in elocution, oratory, gesture, etc. I escaped all that in my boyhood days, and providentially was spared that ruinous torture after I grew up. The way to preach is to preach. Just get full of spirit and truth and turn yourself loose. As a good old brother once expressed it, 'just fill the barrel full, knock the bung out, and let 'er come.' That's the way to preach (Srygley, Larimore and His Boys, p. 150).

Emma Page, in Volume II of Letters and Sermons of T. B. Larimore, tells that a young preacher wrote Larimore asking for advice as to the kind of preaching needed in a protracted meeting. Larimore replied, "Gospel preaching." He went on to say: "Study, work and pray, always doing your very best. No gospel preacher should ever be satisfied to do less than his very best—no one, of course, can do more." In the same volume, Mrs. Larimore writes,

> It may be said that 'preach the word' is T. B. Larimore's motto, so often does he use the expression, in both letters and sermons. He says: 'My position is: Preach the word wheresoever and whensoever Providence directs or duty demands, Always hew to the line, but never hack toes or chop fingers intentionally.'

Srygley said that "they stuck to the Book. They preached neither less nor more than the Bible, and in the very words of the Bible. They looked upon all divisions among professed Christians as not only grave errors, but grievous sins."

Not only did Larimore serve as President and Professor at Mars Hill, he continued to preach, and in doing so he continued to develop his skills as an orator and as one who could touch the hearts of the common man. Time and time again, his contemporaries spoke of his "pathos" in describing his preaching. A term no longer generally used, "pathos" is the emotion of sympathetic pity. T. W. Caskey, in speaking of Larimore, said:

> Often his pathos calls forth tears; but he rarely cries himself. He is not a driveling, crying preacher. He is never sensational in the pulpit; he resorts to no clerical claptrap for effect. He is always deeply in earnest. In social life, he never falls below the dignity of a Christian gentleman; in the pulpit he never falls below the dignity of his sublime theme. His style is simple, dignified and prepossessing; his gestures are easy, graceful and natural. His pronunciation, enunciation and emphasis are perfect.

One of the stories about the sympathetic nature of Larimore is told about a man who had been to hundreds of services and meetings but never responded to the gospel until hearing Larimore speak. When asked why he had not responded to a gospel invitation before, the man replied, "From other preachers I'd learned I was going to hell," he said, "but they seemed pleased that I was. From Larimore I learned I was going to hell, but I could tell it broke his heart to have to tell me so!"

While at Mars Hill, Larimore usually preached every Sunday. During vacation, Larimore traveled extensively and devoted his time to the field of evangelism. The results of his labors and those of his boys were that many churches were established and thousands were brought to Christ.

As Larimore's skill and ability as a preacher grew, so did the number of requests to hold meetings. Larimore became more and more interested in full time evangelism and less and less inclined to continue the college at Mars Hill that had regulated his life for the past eighteen years. Srygley wrote:

> The school declined in interest and patronage, it is true; but only because the immense pressure upon him in pleading letters by every mail to preach the gospel, diverted his attention from the details of college work. More than once have I seen him shed tears over piles of letters begging for preaching when he was confined by college duties at Mars Hill. He would say he had no heart to be there teaching children English Grammar when a perishing world was pleading with him to tell them of Jesus and his love. Those of us who knew his feelings and understood the situation, advised the suspension of the college.

Perhaps the turning point in Larimore's transition to full-time evangelism was the success he experienced in the Nashville meeting of 1885. Srygley said of this meeting: "His success at Nashville in 1885 demonstrated his ability to move great cities as an evangelist." Never before had Larimore preached in a large city, and after giving a commitment to preach in Nashville, he tried earnestly to get out of the commitment. He spoke to David Lipscomb about getting out of his agreement to preach in Nashville, claiming he was inadequate for such an undertaking. Lipscomb refused his request. The meeting began in November and continued about thirty days, resulting in about seventy-five additions to the church. This opened to him a wider field of usefulness, and furnished an additional argument against the expediency of continuing Mars Hill College. Closely following his enlarged usefulness as an evangelist, attendance at Mars Hill College in 1886 was small, and in 1887 discouragingly smaller. In the earlier part of 1887, he had a long letter from a friend and life-long correspondent he greatly loved and in whose judgment he had implicit confidence. His friend strongly urged him to give up the college and devote all of his time to preaching. Larimore finally gave in to the desire of brethren across the nation and to his own desire to preach the gospel full-time.

Closing Mars Hill was a bittersweet time for Larimore, who had devoted such a large part of his life to the college. In summarizing Larimore's work at Mars Hill, Srygley wrote:

> Did ever such a man train such a band of blessed boys for such a grand work with such meager facilities—he and they all alike from the cornfield in the backwoods—without money, without fame, without a support, without a library, encyclopedia, commentary—with no books but God's eternal book of truth? Mars' Hill is a mystery, and her blessed boys a wonder! The wisdom and power of God.

National Evangelist

When Mars Hill closed in 1887, T. B. Larimore was forty-four years old. Though his family was established at the home at Mars Hill, Larimore went everywhere preaching the gospel of Christ—from "Maine to Mexico, from the Carolinas to California"—often being away from home for months at a time. The twenty years after Mars Hill were years of constantly leaving his home and traveling throughout the land to preach the gospel. This must have posed many hardships on his wife, Esther, and their six children, described as "His four sons and two daughters, all baptized by their father in childhood, are intelligent, industrious, exemplary Christians, worthy of the father and mother who have taught them "the good and the right way" (Life, Letters and Sermons of T. B. Larimore, p. 102).

T. B. Larimore at the turn of the twentieth century was a different man than the one turned down by Hopewell church of Christ in 1868 because they thought he might run off prospects. By the turn of the century, he had become the most in-demand preacher in the brotherhood, with more meeting invitations than he could possibly accept. Srygley wrote: "Piles of letters came by every mail pleading for meetings in every part of the country. Later in the year he estimated that the calls for meetings in 1888 would certainly amount in the aggregate to over 360 and probably to 500."

When John T. Brown's, <u>Churches of Christ</u>, appeared in 1904, a chapter in the book was titled, "National Evangelists." The first biography to appear under this heading was that of Theophilus Brown Larimore. The article, written by Selina Holman, describes Larimore:

> Never abusive, rough, or unkind, he is earnest, eloquent, forcible, and always so plain, simple and gentle that little children understand him perfectly and love him devotedly. He has a vivid imagination, loves the beautiful, the innocent and the pure, and possesses an unrivaled gift of language. He avoids all slang, pulpit profanity, affectation and ecclesiastical titles. He speaks evil of none, is envious of none, and considers himself no better than the humblest of his brethren. He is marvelously magnetic. To know him is to love him. To call him brother is a pleasure. He has hosts of friends, loyal and true. He is loved by men, women, and children, as few have ever been loved. He is never willing to preach less than twice every day and three times on Sunday, and prefers to preach three times every day. While he goes home as often as he can, he tries to never deliver less than 700 discourses a year. He adapts himself to all sorts of circumstances—becomes 'all things to all men'—but he is averse to short meetings, because he believes the longer they are the better they are.

Brown's book mentions, in particular, the meeting at Sherman, Texas, Larimore's longest meeting. This meeting began on January 3, 1894 and closed on June 7, lasting five months and four days. During this meeting, he preached three hundred and thirty-three sermons, preaching twice every day and three times every Sunday and there were 331 additions to the church during the meeting.

While Larimore was engaged in this protracted meeting, his friend and confidant, F. D. Srygley wrote to him asking about the progress of the meeting, its probable length — it had then been in progress nine weeks — how the preacher could stand such long continued work, and how and where he found material for sermons. Larimore wrote back that the interest was increasing daily and that he was holding up well. He wrote: "Nothing can be better for me than to preach twice every day and three times on Sunday, unless it is to preach three times every day and Sunday too. He stated that his voice was holding up and that no mortal knew when the meeting would end." He told F. D. that subjects and material for sermons were inexhaustible. "The Bible," he said, "is full of themes and thoughts and truths." He said he would exhaust Bible themes "when swallows drink the ocean dry."

When asked what books he consulted, he replied, "The Bible, Webster's Dictionary and the Bible—these three, and no more." When questioned how long his fight would last in Sherman, he replied, "Till mustered out of service."

T. B. Larimore established rules to live by, and these rules certainly became a part of his preaching. On December 31, 1895, Larimore wrote a letter to F. D. Srygley from Columbia, Tennessee. He wrote:

> Instead of writing you a new-year letter, as I have so often done, I write you, as follows, a few of my life rules, as they occur to me in the light of the last day of 1895— rules which I hope to strictly observe, both in letter and spirit, till God shall call me home: (1) Be kind; (2) be meek; (3) be true; (4) be humble; (5) be gentle; (6) be polite; (7) be patient; (8) be earnest; (9) be careful; (10) be hopeful; (11) be faithful; (12) be cheerful; (13) be grateful; (14) be generous; (15) be prayerful; (16) be courteous; (17) be unselfish; (18) be thoughtful; (19) be industrious; (20) be consecrated; (21) be conscientious; (22) always 'do the right;' (23) do as much good as possible; (24) do as little evil as possible; (25) eat to live, not live to

eat; (26) if possible, be perfectly pure; (27) if not, be pure as possible; (28) always make the best of the situation; (29) be clean— body, soul, and spirit— clean in thought, in word, in deed— always clean; (30) conscientiously consecrate all to Christ— head, hand, heart— body, soul, spirit— time, tongue, talent— mind, muscle, money— consecrate all to Him who gave his very life to ransom a recreant, lost, and ruined race.

One of the things that characterized T. B. Larimore was his aversion to conflict. His non-combative nature was recognized in his refusal to debate and take positions on issues over which churches of Christ were fighting at the time. He refused to take sides on the instrumental music in worship issue and the church sponsored society issue. Though he had opinions, he believed he did not have the right to impose them on others. This caused Larimore problems with the liberals and conservatives of the day—the liberals accusing him of being too conservative and the conservatives accusing him of not having backbone to stand firmly on the issues dividing the church. J. M. Powell, in his book, The Man From Mars Hill, quotes from a personal letter from S. P. Pitman telling of Larimore preaching in a meeting in Hickman County, Tennessee. He wrote:

> Before closing the service, brother Larimore asked whether anyone had something to say. This preacher arose and began to argue. He said, 'Brother Larimore said so and so, but my Bible says otherwise.' When there was a lull, brother Larimore said, 'Is that all?' 'Yes,' the man replied. Then Larimore said calmly, 'Let us stand and be dismissed.'

The Later Years

By the year 1910, brother Larimore's life had undergone a number of changes. The children had grown up. Toppie,

(T. B., Jr.) a doctor, had died in 1903 at the age of thirty-one. In 1907, his wife, Esther, died and was laid to rest next to Toppie in the Gresham Cemetery across the road from the Larimore home and a couple of hundred feet from the baptizing hole near the newly constructed church at Mars Hill. As family ties were unraveling and demands for preaching were greater than ever, T. B. spent even less time at Mars Hill than he had for the past twenty years of full-time evangelism. On January 1, 1911, he married Miss Emma Page, a godly Christian woman, well-educated by Charlotte Fanning (the wife of T. B.'s old professor, Tolbert Fanning). Emma was a writer and a stenographer. By the time of their marriage, Emma Page had already edited two volumes of Larimore's sermons. For years, people had asked brother Larimore to tell them again what he had said in his sermons, and he could never do it. Emma Page could record the sermons as Larimore spoke and transcribe them so that the entire world could read the sermons of T. B. Larimore, recorded in three volumes. The first volume was <u>Life, Letters and Sermons of T. B. Larimore</u> by F. D. Srygley. Volumes two and three were <u>Letters and Sermons of T. B. Larimore</u> by Emma Page. These volumes are rich with the poetic qualities of the master wordsmith. This writer would like to share two samples of Larimore's ability to paint pictures with words.

The Church of Christ

Kingdoms may be founded, may flourish and may fall; but the church of Christ can never fall, can never fail. Atheism may assail, infidelity may sneer, skepticism may smile and anxious hearts may fear for the safety of Zion but Zion stands secure, backed by the promise of the great I Am that it shall never be destroyed, the literal, living, abiding fulfillment of the promise of the Lord Jesus Christ: 'Upon this rock I will build my church and the gates of hell shall not prevail against it.' The sun may be blotted out, the moon cease to reflect light, the stars may fall from the withering vault of night, and the heavens be rolled up like a scroll, and the wreck of matter and the crash of the worlds may come and the judgment day be set; but, when the angel of the Lord shall descend on pinions dipped in the love light enveloping the throne of God and, planting one foot upon the sea and rides upon the storm that time was, time is, but time shall be no more—even then the church of Christ shall stand, secure as the throne of God itself: for our Savior promised long ago, 'the gates of hell shall not prevail against it;' and Jehovah hath declared 'it shall never be destroyed;' and the Holy Spirit by the pen of Isaiah, the prophet, says: 'The word of our God shall stand forever': so then, whether we stand or fall, whether we do right or wrong, whether we are saved or lost, the church of Christ shall stand, having been built upon this immovable foundation.

The Rock

Caesarea was founded upon a mass of imperishable rock. It was built of stone, from hovel to palace, from foundation to roof, hence might well have been called the 'Rock City,' or the 'City of Rocks.' It was surrounded by a stone wall—high, massive, strong—an effective means of protection for a town in that far-away-age of the world. It was situated in one of the roughest, rockiest, most romantic, picturesque and rugged spots on earth, at the foot of Mount Hermon, that cast its dense, dark shadow upon the town for hours at the beginning of every bright day, and near the head of the rolling Jordan, that leaped from the bosom of the earth and flashed and sparkled as it swept on its course to the depths of the mysterious Dead Sea. Just about one mile toward the golden gates of the morning from Caesarea Philippi, resting upon one of the rocky spurs of Mount Hermon, was a rock fortress considered absolutely impregnable in that age of the world antedating the use of nitroglycerin, gunpowder, dynamite, guncotton and other explosives that are used in the modern science of human slaughter, that provision being made that, in the event an enemy should break down the walls around the city, the inhabitants might flee to that rock fortress and be safe.

It was in the coasts or immediate presence of this rock founded, rock-builded, rock-bounded, rock-surrounded, rock-protected, rock-shadowed city that Jesus, the Rock of Ages, the Rock for sinners cleft, said to Peter, the 'rock'-Cephas, the 'stone'-in reference to that spiritual institution that had been represented by Daniel, in the then long ago, as a little rock cut out of the mountain without hands and subsequently filling the whole earth; that spiritual institution every member of which is called in the Bible a 'lively stone' or a 'living stone:' 'Upon this rock I will build my church; and the gates of hell shall not prevail against it.'

There is nothing accidental about the phraseology of the Bible, nothing any more accidental about the framing of any picture we find hanging upon the walls of the temple of truth than there is about the painting of that picture by the hand of Omnipotence itself. So we should rejoice that this wonderful picture is presented to us in framework rendered sublimely attractive, and we should appreciate not only the picture, but the very framing of that picture, shaded by towering mountains seeming to pierce the heavens bending in blue beauty above them, in which the hand of Jehovah has hung the picture upon the walls of his temple of truth divine.

After Mars Hill, T. B. Larimore was not only recognized as a great preacher but as a great educator as well. He was offered the presidency at several colleges, which he refused. His love was in evangelism. He had given twenty years of his life to education. The rest of his days would be spent preaching the gospel of Christ. T. B. and Emma traveled the continent. Hundreds of meetings were held, and thousands obeyed the gospel as a result of his labors. He and Emma finally decided to settle in California. They moved to

Berkeley, California, before moving to Santa Ana, California. Larimore remained there until his death in 1929.

The May 16, 1929 issue of *Gospel Advocate* contained testimonials by N. B. Hardeman, Mrs. T. B. Larimore, T. Q. Martin, G. W. Riggs, M. C. Kurfees, A. G. Freed, E. N. Glenn, A. M. Burton, James H. Sewell, J. G. Allen, Mrs. A. N. Killebrew, J. Pettey Ezell, H. Leo Boles, S. H. Hall, F. W. Smith, F. B. Srygley, Andy T. Ritchie, Sr., Foy E. Wallace, Jr., W. S. Long, G.P.H. Showalter, F. L. Rowe, Wayne W. Burton, and J. Madison Wright.

The May 23rd issue of *Gospel Advocate* contained testimonials by G. C. Brewer, E. N. Glenn, E. C. Fuqua, Gentry Reynolds, Earnest Beam, Thomas E. Milholland, Robert S. King, L. C. Wilkerson, F. C. Sowell, and J. D. Clemons.

The thirty-three articles contained in these two issues of *Gospel Advocate* provide great insight as to how T. B. Larimore touched the lives of so many. Several writers contemporary with brother Larimore mentioned that Larimore had a special way with little children—that they absolutely adored him. It is interesting that Mrs. Larimore's article was titled, *Mr. Larimore and His Little Friends*. In this article she wrote:

> Mr. Larimore's life and works would not be complete without mention of his friends among children. He loved children, always and everywhere, and in the various places where he lived even a brief time there are children and young people who were devoted to him and whom he loved very tenderly. He appreciated a baby's being named for him, and appreciated especially his voluntary namesakes—children who voluntarily added 'Larimore' to the name already bestowed by parents.

In the May 16, 1929 issue of *Gospel Advocate*, a story titled, "Noted Divine Answers Call" (a reprint of a *Nashville*

Banner article), extolled the accomplishments of T. B. Larimore, saying:

> That he was personally known to more people than any other man in the brotherhood from this long period of service and that he had preached more sermons than any other men living was the claim frequently made by religious authors, some of whom also advanced the claim that he had probably baptized more people than any minister of the church of Christ for nearly one hundred years.

The article mentioned the accomplishments of men like William Hayden, Walter Scott, Benjamin Franklin (who had baptized more than 10,000), and John Allen Gano (who had baptized approximately 10,000). The article made it plain that it was believed that T. B. Larimore had surpassed the accomplishments of these great men.

T. B. Larimore had become a household name in families of Christians throughout the nation. His ability to preach was second to none. He was an orator and a wordsmith of the highest order. One of the great compliments paid to brother Larimore in the May 16th issue of *Gospel Advocate* was made by T. Q. Martin, when he wrote:

> T. B. Larimore was both grand and eloquent. He was an orator of the rare type, truly an eloquent man. To my mind, one of the greatest things in the life of this man of God is the fact that later in life he suppressed his oratorical powers, lest people might be moved by his oratory rather than the word of God.

Such was the preacher, T. B. Larimore.

Mars Hill College

Chapter 24

"Parson" George Ricks

The story of "Parson" George Ricks is one of a man overcoming almost insurmountable odds. George Ricks was born a slave and died a landowner, respected citizen, and admired gospel preacher. George was born in 1835, sometime after his master, Abraham Ricks, moved into what is now Colbert County, Alabama, and began construction on his plantation, in the Spring Valley community known as "The Oaks."

Abraham Ricks

Abraham Ricks was born October 16, 1791, in Halifax County, North Carolina. He married his first cousin, Charlotte B. Forte. Abraham and Charlotte Ricks moved to Alabama about 1820 with thirty other families, bringing all their possessions including slaves. For awhile, they lived in Lawrence County, Alabama, and then moved to Colbert County in 1825. At this time, Ricks began construction of his plantation home, "The Oaks." The house was completed in 1832 and stands today as an example of an early plantation home. Abraham Ricks owned about 10,000 acres of land and 300 slaves. He was also the principal owner of a new investment at that time—a railroad. The Tuscumbia, Courtland & Decatur Railroad was the first railroad in the south. Stretching about forty miles from Tuscumbia to Decatur, this railroad served the need for transportation between the communities where river traffic on the Tennessee River was impossible due to the shoals in the Tennessee River between Elk River and Cypress Creek.

Abraham Ricks was a Christian, having obeyed the gospel before coming to Alabama. Evidently interested in spiritual matters, Abraham provided for the slaves on his plantation an opportunity to develop spiritually and to worship God without hindrance from outsiders. His son, Abraham Ricks, Jr., was sent to be educated by Alexander Campbell, at Bethany College in Bethany, Virginia. He was graduated "First Class of Merit" in 1848. He was a classmate of the famous gospel preacher, J. W. McGarvey.

Ricks was concerned about the treatment of slaves on his property. His granddaughter, Miss Bertie Ricks, reminisced about her family at "The Oaks" in an article published in 1936, written by Shartie Lane. Miss Bertie Ricks

George Ricks worked on the plantation known as "The Oaks." Pictured is the plantation home today.

lived at "The Oaks" until her death in 1960. She stated that her grandfather "was a kind man and a level headed practical business man." She said he was "a lenient master and his servants were devoted to him. He had overseers about the plantation but he never allowed them to whip the slaves." She said her grandfather did whip one slave for brutally beating his wife and another who threatened his (Abraham Ricks) wife, Charlotte. She said "my grandfather never separated a man and his wife and my father never sold any of his slaves." Bertie Ricks also stated that the slaves "were all well fed, clothed and housed. The old plantation used to ring with their laughter and their songs. And they were happy for many of them have told me so. Indeed one old man cried when freedom came and begged my father not to free him." She also said that Abraham Ricks gave each of the slaves "an acre of ground to make a crop of their own and to do with the proceeds as they pleased." This is said not to justify slavery, but to point out that slaves at "The Oaks" fared much better than the slaves on most other plantations.

Charlotte Ricks was a special lady. She was described as an unusually lovable character and an angel of mercy. Her obituary appeared in the March 26, 1874 issue of the *North Alabamian* newspaper (whose editor was Captain A. H. Keller, father of Helen Keller) and was one of the longest obituaries ever printed by the paper. The article spoke extensively of her love for and ability to grow flowers. The obituary went on to say, "She was truly a ministering angel to her family and friends, possessing a mind unusually bright, a clear judgment, and a heart that knew not evil. Every virtue found a home in her heart, and made her loved and lovely." The obituary extolled her virtues in many areas, including hospitality, stating: "For two generations her name has been the synonym of hospitality in this community. And where has such hospitality ever been excelled?"

Charlotte Rick's concern for others extended to the slaves on the plantation. Her granddaughter said, "Many of our servants were taught to read and write. My grandmother would teach the little house Negroes the Catechism on Sundays after she had sent them home for their mothers to bathe and dress them."

It was probably in these Bible classes that a young George Ricks developed a love for the Word of God and determined to become a gospel preacher. Later, as a man, George Ricks would become a leader in the black community, loved and respected by both races. George probably learned to read and write at the feet of Charlotte Ricks.

A church was built on the plantation for the slaves. It is not known when the church at The Oaks began. The sign in front of the present building states 1832. If this is the case, the Christian Home Church of Christ is the oldest church of Christ in Colbert and Franklin County. (Franklin County was divided into Colbert and Franklin after the Civil War.) This would also be one of oldest churches of Christ built by and owned by black brethren anywhere in the country. There is evidence that the slaves were meeting on the plantation in the years prior to the Civil War. However, the first known meetinghouse was a log building built by Abraham Ricks, Jr. This building would have probably been built after the death of Abraham Ricks, Sr. in 1852.

George Ricks was a hard worker. A marker at the Ricks Cemetery where George is buried states that he was:

> [A] slave to Abraham Ricks (and) he became the first black land owner in North Alabama by planting cotton on Saturday evenings and picking it by the moon light. He sold his cotton and with the proceeds bought fifty-three acres of land. His landholding would increase by another seventy acres. He was the first African-American to pay property taxes in Franklin County, Alabama.

George Ricks' love for the truth motivated him to preach the gospel. Brother Ricks traveled extensively to preach, riding on a bay mule to preaching appointments. Some of his preaching appointments were over one hundred miles away. *The History of the Tuscumbia Church of Christ* stated that "Parson" George Ricks, in 1880, "preached for the Rock

Creek Church of Christ, near Tuscumbia, Alabama." This is the church that had its beginning in 1868 under the influence of James and Sarah Srygley, the parents of F. B. and F. D. Srygley, famous preachers after the Civil War. This would have been highly unusual for a black man to preach in a "white" church. Evidently, Ricks was so respected among the white brethren that he was allowed to preach the gospel in their churches.

On many preaching trips, George was usually accompanied by Albert Eggleston. When asked why he went with brother Ricks, Eggleston said that George was a plain spoken man and feared that George might be attacked by his hearers. Eggleston said, "I went along to do his fighting for him!" Although Eggleston heard the gospel preached many times, he never obeyed it. He did request that Marshall Keeble, a very well-known black preacher in churches of Christ, speak at his funeral. Keeble honored his request, coming to the CME church in Tuscumbia, Alabama, to speak at his funeral. Mr. Eggleston died in 1950 at about the age of 100 years.

"Parson" George began preaching about 1867 or 1868. At this time, the church meeting on "The Oaks" was undergoing a financial crisis. Even though Miss Bertie Ricks reported that her father, Abraham Ricks, Jr., had built the building, there must have been indebtedness for the building materials owed by the members of the Christian Home Church of Christ. The Ricks family experienced economic devastation from the war. Mrs. Charlotte Ricks told how the Yankees had taken off all her mules and horses. She said Abe (Abraham Ricks, Jr.) was plowing with steers while she had nothing with which to plow, but intended to put her cows to the plow as soon as she could get them broke to the plow. Charlotte Ricks said she might as well laugh as cry over her troubles. The slave labor was gone and also the work animals. A once profitable plantation of 10,000 acres was reduced to what could be plowed by family members without animals broken to the plow. In these hard economic times, cash was hard to come by.

This scarcity of cash and probable "call of debt" prompted "Parson" George to take the leadership in securing money to pay off the debt on the church building. On December 20, 1867, he wrote a letter soliciting help to pay for the newly constructed house of worship on the old plantation. He asked Dr. Edmund Chisholm of Tuscumbia, Alabama to help him write a letter to Edmund's brother, Dr. L. C. Chisholm, for this purpose. David Lipscomb printed the letter in the January 2, 1868 issue of the <u>Gospel Advocate</u>. It is as follows:

> Letter from a Colored Brother—Help Wanted.
> Tuscumbia, Ala., Dec. 20, 1867.
> Dr Chisholm: —After saying howdy to you, I will state that I am doing very well, preaching at my old mistress Ricks', and have about fifty members, and at my last baptising (sic), which was this day three weeks ago, I baptised three members into the church of Christ. So you see we are well with the excepting of need of money. We have not yet paid for our church-house. Supposing that a there may be some colored brethren in the vicinity in which you live belonging to the Christian ranks, who are not so poor as we are, and who are willing to devote a small amount, be it ever so little, I write to give you the fact that we are in need of money to pay the amount we are behind on our church-house. Will you please show this also to the white brethren—Brother Fanning and others, and ask their aid in the matter? If you can do anything for us, we will be thankful. Howbeit, let me hear immediately, say by Christmas, what you have done for us.
>
> Direct your letter to me in care of your brother, Dr. Ed. Chisholm, at Tuscumbia. We are obliged to raise as much as twenty or twenty-five dollars by Christmas, if we possibly can. I hope and trust you will be successful enough to do it.

Yours in Christ, George Ricks

David Lipscomb immediately responded by writing:

> We have the assurance from Brother Chisholm and others that Brother Geo. Ricks is a most worthy, unassuming brother, and is doing a good and faithful work for the Lord and his people. We learn the Church at Franklin College has furnished Brother George with the amount he asks for immediately, but other small remittances, as above, to Dr. E. Chisholm would be most worthily appropriated. We are very anxious to aid all efforts to Christianize and elevate the negro and prepare him for living usefully here and hereafter.

"Parson" George is mentioned again in the *Gospel Advocate*, this time in the April 29, 1885 issue. He was visiting or preaching in the Nashville area and came by the *Gospel Advocate* office. Brother Lipscomb wrote:

> Eld. Joe (sic, evidently meant Geo.) Ricks, (colored) of Spring Valley, Ala., gave us a call last week. He has been preaching about seventeen years during which time he has baptized about 300 hundred (sic) persons. His home congregation, Christian Home, Colbert county (sic), Ala., numbers 96 members and besides him there are six preachers. There is also a church at Fayettville, Talladaga county, with 49 members that Bro. Ricks has been mainly instrumental in building up.

From humble beginnings, the little church on The Oaks plantation grew from Bible classes taught by Charlotte Ricks to the point of having a building in which to meet. When George Ricks gave an acre of his property to the church for the construction of the building, the Christian Home Church of Christ had a place to meet. Miss Bertie Ricks said in the article:

Later, sometime before the Civil War, my father built a little log church for his Negroes and as it was the first church of that kind established among the Negroes they named it the 'Mother church' and those that have been established since are called the 'Branches.' My father let his servants hold their services to suit themselves. They could preach, shout and sing as much as they wished so long as they conducted themselves with decorum and no one was allowed to molest them or to go there in derision. The land was donated by a slave of my father's who accumulated quite a bit of property nearby after the war. Taught by my father as best he knew, this Negro was the preacher until his death and was much revered among his own people and highly respected among the white.

Christian Home Church

This much revered and highly respected Negro preacher was Parson George Ricks. A man, who by hard work, secured his own property, gained an education, and became a gospel preacher. George Ricks traveled a great deal, preaching among the black people, converted several hundred, and influenced thousands for good in his lifetime.

The building of the Christian Home Church of Christ was also used as a gathering place for the residents of the community and as a schoolhouse for many years, where grades kindergarten through the ninth grade held classes. Ms. Opheia Coffee served as teacher before 1931. In that year, Ms. Beatrice Sykes became the teacher. After a couple of years, Virginia Mayes became the teacher. In 1934, Lozzie Steele came and taught for one year. Lastly, Joe

Griffin's mother taught until 1937 when the school closed. Some of the students of the Ricks School were Sadie Cobb (future wife of Huston Cobb and elder at Westside Church of Christ, who assisted in this research), Abie Sledge, Frankie Mullins Davis, Alfred Mullins, Gladys Mullins, Marvin Ricks, Susan McClam, J. B. and Ellis Marvin, George D. Sledge, Rosie Vinson, Emma Jean King-White, Mattie Crawley-Gunn, and Otelia Long.

In the 1940s, the old log cabin where the saints met at the Christian Home Church of Christ was showing signs of age. The floors rotted and time, termites, and weather took a toll on the old building. Brother Fred Ricks, Sr., with the help of his son, Fred, Jr., and his daughters, Mildred Ricks Smith and Lois Ricks King, began to gather rocks and stones from nearby fields to raise the floor. Then concrete was poured for a more permanent foundation. Percy Ricks, Fred Ricks, Sr., Fred Ricks, Jr., John Lee Ricks, and Rave Randolph worked to build the block structure that stands today. The old building's roof and ceiling were retained in the new structure.

Brother T. W. Rucks (1896-1984) carried on services every 4th Sunday after leaving High Street Church of Christ in Tuscumbia, Alabama. Brother Rucks was born in Wilson County, Tennessee, and attended public school in Lebanon, Tennessee. He attended Nashville Christian Institute and later attended International Bible College. He began his preaching career in Nashville in 1920. He moved to Florence, Alabama, and in 1933 became the minister of the East Alabama Street Church of Christ, which is now the Westside Church of Christ. Brother Rucks also served as minister at High Street, Christian Home, Cherokee Church of Christ, and Reedtown Church of Christ. He continued to preach at Christian Home until his death. He would catch the bus in Tuscumbia and travel to the old store on Highway 20, and brother Fred Ricks, Sr. would meet him in a wagon pulled by a team of mules and bring him to the building at Christian Home.

When brother Rucks died, the services at Christian Home Church of Christ ceased. However, the church has begun to meet again in recent years, with John Smalley as the preacher. Brother Smalley's wife, Delores Long Smalley, is a direct descendant of "Parson" George Ricks. Another descendant of George Ricks, Percy Ricks, helped this writer with research for this story.

From his labors in establishing and building up the Christian Home Church of Christ in the Spring Valley community of Colbert County, Alabama, on what is known as "The Oaks" plantation, several churches of Christ have been established in North Alabama. So many churches came from the Christian Home Church of Christ that Christian Home became known as The Mother Church. The Mother Church gave birth to several congregations. These include High Street Church of Christ in Tuscumbia, Cherokee Church of Christ in Cherokee, Sterling Boulevard Church of Christ in Sheffield, Westside Church of Christ in Leighton, Reedtown Church of Christ in Russellville, and a church at Fayetteville in Talladega, Alabama.

When "Parson" George died, an obituary appeared in *The Leighton News*, Friday, January 1, 1909. The obituary said:

> Rev. George Ricks
> A Tribute to a Faithful Colored Man.
> Rev. George Ricks, colored, seventy-three years of age*, died December 25, 1908. As the angels of God sang out on the Christmas air, 'Glory to God in the highest, and on earth peace, good-will toward men,' the summons came to him—'Come unto me, all ye who are weary and heavy laden, and I will give you rest.'
> He laid down his cross and took up his crown.
> Parson George, as he was familiarly known, like Joshua, was a good fighter for the right. His characteristics were honesty, truthfulness, generosity, freedom of religious thought, and faith in the eternal God. Early in life, he began work in his

Master's vineyard. He was never happier than on the Sabbath days when he could gather his people together to sing the songs of Zion and tell of Jesus and His love.

He has sung his last doxology, but to his flock and large family of sons and daughters, weep not, but walk in his footsteps, so on the other shore you may clasp hands and sing hallelujah.

"Parson" George Ricks was a great servant of God. From humble beginnings to highly respected community and church leader, George Ricks is a man to whom honor is due.

*According to the obituary, George Ricks would have been born in 1835. However, his tombstone states that he was born in 1838.

Grave of "Parson" George Ricks

Chapter 25

The Murder of James Madison Pickens

Perhaps one of the greatest news stories in the history of Lawrence County, Alabama, was reported in the local newspaper, The *Moulton Advertiser*, February 10, 1881. The extremely short account of the murder may have been due to the newspaper's editor's distaste for the victim. The murdered man was one of the most well-known citizens of Lawrence County. He was a gospel preacher, principal of a private school (which he owned), editor of a paper, and a recent candidate for governor in the 1880 governor's election, on the Greenback Party ticket, only to be defeated in the polls. The murdered man was James Madison Pickens. The *Moulton Advertiser* published the following:

> Robert G. Letson shot and killed Rev. J. M. Pickens and severely if not fatally wounded Wm. Davidson, at Mountain Home, on Thursday morning of last week. Letson immediately repaired to Courtland and surrendered himself to the authorities, stating that he had killed Pickens and Davidson— Davidson for slandering his daughter, and Pickens in self-defense. He was given a preliminary trial at Courtland on Saturday and Monday last, and the following card tells of the result: Courtland, Ala., Feb. 7th 1881. Maj. D. C. White: Dear Sir: Letson's trial was concluded this evening. The attorneys submitted the case without argument. The verdict was to send him to Tuscumbia jail, there to await his trial in the Circuit Court. Letson preferred jail to giving bond. The Sheriff will take him there tomorrow. No other news. Your friend, D. Simmons

The murder was reported in several other papers in nearby cities with much more detail. Jourd White, one of the editors of the *Moulton Advertiser*, was a political enemy of J. M. Pickens. This is probably the reason the news story was given such little space in the local paper. Only a few months prior to his death, Pickens was known statewide as the Greenback Party candidate for governor. At the time of his death and in recent years, speculation has been that the death of J. M. Pickens was not an accident or in self-defense, as claimed by Robert Letson, but a political assassination.

J. M. Pickens was in his prime, only forty-four years old when he died. (He died three days prior to his forty-fifth birthday.) He was one of the finest gospel preachers and debaters among the Disciples. Mrs. Alexander Campbell was so moved by Pickens' preaching ability that while living near Mountain Home in Lawrence County, Alabama, she presented Pickens with Alexander Campbell's personal Bible.

Early Life

James Madison Pickens was born February 6, 1836, in Maury County, Tennessee. He was the third child of William and Charlotte Bruce Pickens. Young Pickens was an excellent student, learning Latin and Greek during his leisure time. He attended Jackson College at Columbia, Tennessee, and then went to the University of Kentucky at Lexington. Although Pickens did not graduate from this institution, he continued studying on his own. To his knowledge of the languages of Latin and Greek, he added Hebrew. For his day in the South, he was considered a scholar.

Pickens was brought up in the church of Christ (also referred to as The Disciples and/or the Christian Church). Perhaps his early years of spiritual training were at the feet of men like Tolbert Fanning, John M. Barnes, and James Anderson, who were men who preached in Maury County prior to the Civil War.

When the Civil War broke out, Pickens enlisted in the Confederate Army on August 28, 1861, at Camp Galloway, Columbia, Tennessee. He was a private in Captain Edmund O'Neill's company, 2nd Regiment, Tennessee Volunteers, and subsequently Company B, 2nd Regiment, Robison's Regiment, Tennessee Infantry. When his enlistment was up, he enlisted for two more years. This was on February 14, 1862, three weeks prior to the Battle of Shiloh. For some unknown reason, Pickens was discharged on April 4, 1862, at Corinth, Mississippi, just two days before the beginning of the Battle of Shiloh. Since the South was preparing for the greatest battle yet in the war, there must have been a reason for this discharge. Every able-bodied man was needed in this battle. The assumption is that Pickens had taken sick or was injured and not able to fight in the battle.

Pickens was described as a talented musician, who played the violin. While in the Confederate army, Pickens became associated with Carlo Patti, a brother of the famous singer Adelina Patti, and they performed concerts to raise money for the Confederate hospitals.

War brings out the worst in men, and moved by the immorality of the troops, Pickens began to speak to them of spiritual matters and tried to preach to them. The soldiers didn't care for Pickens' preaching, and on one occasion, Pickens was quoted as saying, "If you fellows don't want to listen to me you can just go to hell and be damned!"

Pickens in Lawrence County, Alabama

After the war, Pickens married Mary Caroline Williams of Columbus, Mississippi. They bought a school and farm at Mountain Home, Lawrence County, Alabama. According to a paper written by J. M. Pickens' son in the Disciples of Christ Historical Society archives, "the farm consisted of 300 to 400 acres. It was on the top of a low mountain that overlooked the Tennessee Valley to the north." The location was described as a beautiful natural location, a few miles south of the Tennessee River and four miles south of the Memphis and Charleston Railroad, the nearest station being Wheeler Station, named for General Joseph Wheeler, whose plantation at Pond Spring was nearby. The Pickens family lived a few miles from the Barclay's Ingleside Plantation. Dr. Judson J. Barclay would later be listed as a co-editor of the paper that Pickens started. Pickens' paper began about 1870. He edited the *Christian Monthly*, which became the *Southern Christian Weekly* and continued for four or five years.

Mountain Home School

For several years, J. M. Pickens conducted his school at Mountain Home. It began about 1867, and lasted until after his death when Mrs. Pickens sold the school to a group of Quakers, who continued the school several years. An old photograph shows the main building of the school, a two story structure, sometime in the 1950s, according to the model of the automobile that is parked in front of it. The building no longer stands.

This writer has a copy of the August 1870 edition of the *Southern Christian Weekly*, obtained from the Disciples of Christ Historical Society, Nashville, Tennessee, which carried an advertisement for Mountain Home School. It stated:

> The next session of this School will begin on Monday, October 3d, 1870 and continue nine months, embracing two terms of eighteen weeks each.
>
> LOCATION—This Institution is located in Lawrence County, Alabama, on the mountain south of the Tennessee Valley, near the Memphis and Charleston Railroad, seven miles Southeast of Courtland, and immediately on the road from Courtland to Moulton.
>   The situation combines every advantage which Nature can give to render it eligible for a School;

pure, fresh air, free from miasma, dust and all local causes of sickness, and abundance of excellent spring water, pure freestone and chalybeate, furnished by a number of beautiful, gushing springs; is quiet, retired, free from all temptations to extravagance and vice, and has long been a favorite resort for persons seeking health.

BUILDINGS—The buildings were originally constructed for a school, are sufficiently extensive for the accommodation of one hundred pupils, and are well adapted to school purposes.

COURSE OF STUDY—The Course of Study will embrace every branch of education usually taught in schools of high grade and necessary to prepare the student for any business or position in life. Particular attention will be given to the elementary principles of an English education, while as extensive a course of Mathematics, of Latin and of Greek will be furnished as may be desired. The best facilities for learning Modern Languages and Music will be afforded.

Strict discipline will be maintained at all times, and every endeavor used to induce studious and industrious habits, moral conduct and genteel deportment. Each boarding pupil will be expected to attend worship and Sunday School regularly.

BOARDING—A regular boarding department will be kept up in connection with the School; everything necessary to health and comfort will be furnished and served in good style, and an earnest endeavor will be made to remove all cause of complaint so frequently and so justly urged against boarding schools.

RATE OF CHARGES

Board, including lodging, washing, lights and fuel, per month	$20.00
Tuition in Primary Department, per month	3.00
Tuition in Preparatory Department, per month	4.00
Tuition in Academic Department, per month	5.00
Music, extra per month	5.00

Use of Instrument, extra per month   1.00
Modern Languages, extra per month   2.00
No extra charge for any branch of study except for Modern Languages and Music.

FACULTY
J. M. Pickens, Principal and Teacher of Rhetoric, Mental and Moral Philosophy, Latin and Greek.

Mrs. M. M. Pickens, Composition, Rhetoric and Music

W. M. Wood, English Branches and Mathematics

Mrs. Sarah E. Williams, Matron
Other competent assistants will be secured as the demand may require.

Male and Female Departments conducted separately.

Persons coming to Mountain Home should stop at Courtland, on the Memphis and Charleston Railroad, where arrangements will be made for conveyance at reasonable rates.

Address the undersigned, Mountain Home, via Courtland, Ala.
        J. M. Pickens, Principal

In 1868, Pickens asked a young teacher to join him at Mountain Home School. This young teacher, fresh out of Franklin College, was T. B. Larimore. Larimore, recognizing the influence of schools like Pickens' school, started his own school in 1871 near Florence, Alabama. Larimore's school at Mars Hill lasted from 1871 to 1887, and had a great influence on the preaching of the gospel and establishing of churches in Northwest Alabama. Hundreds of young men were educated and trained to preach at this school.

Larimore's marriage ceremony was performed by J. M. Pickens on August 30, 1868, as T. B. married Julia Esther Gresham. Esther had inherited twenty-eight acres of land from her father, Philemon Gresham. On this initial acreage, T. B. and Esther labored to establish a college that would eventually have over five hundred acres and twenty buildings.

Controversy between the Tuscumbia Baptists and the church of Christ

Some of J. M. Pickens' earliest preaching in Northwest Alabama was at Tuscumbia, Alabama. In 1866, Pickens held a meeting in Tuscumbia and helped to establish the church that had been devastated during the Civil War. The Tuscumbia church was organized under the leadership of Dr. W. H. Wharton in 1834. Dr. L. C. Chisholm of Tuscumbia wrote in the *Gospel Advocate* the following note:

> During the last winter our young brother, J. M. Pickens, rather accidentally visited Tuscumbia, where he very soon assembled a little flock that seemed both willing and anxious to keep the ordinances of the Lord, but at that time it seemed next to impossibility to get a hearing, but the scale has now turned .... We are steadily gaining ground and adding to our number, but the labors of Bro. Pickens have not been confined to Tuscumbia alone, (he preaches at other places as well). We had the pleasure of visiting Moulton, Ala., in company with him last week, and a more interesting meeting we never witnessed. The interest seemed to increase to the very close. The people seemed to be spellbound and taken captive by the majesty and force of the truth. The church that formerly met at that place, was most effectually aroused from its lethargy, the erring reclaimed and sinners came flocking to the

fold. We were particularly struck with seeing an old gray-headed veteran from the Baptists come forward, give his hand and hear him say he had earnestly sought the truth for twenty-five years, and it had dawned upon him at last. Bro. P. labored faithfully with us, and promises to continue his labors in North Alabama, Mississippi and West Tennessee. Will the brethren in these sections sustain him, and ...all who labor with and for us in the Lord (*Gospel Advocate*, Sept. 11, 1866)?

Prior to the war, the church in Tuscumbia had secured property and built a nice brick meetinghouse. Evidently, dispersed and devastated by the war, the church stopped meeting in the building. At some point, the Baptists of Tuscumbia took the building for their meeting place. Pickens tried to find legal documents giving the Baptists the right to the building, but could not. Not only were the Baptists meeting in the building for which they had no legal documents to prove ownership, the church of Christ was not allowed to use the building.

In June 1870, Pickens wrote an article in *The Christian Monthly* pointing out that the building under question still belonged to the Church of Christ. He was answered by Joseph Shackelford of Tuscumbia, speaking on behalf of the Baptists, and Shackelford's answer was printed in the August, 1870 issue of *The Christian Monthly*. Shackelford contended that the building came into the hands of Mr. Carroll, a citizen of Tuscumbia. Shackelford stated, "How he became the owner of the house or had a right to sell it we are unable to say." He continued, "At any rate, he sold it to Deacon Edmund Ellet, a member and deacon of the Baptist church, for $500.00."

Pickens responded to Shackelford, saying, "We object, however, to at least two dozen of his statements." Pickens said, "Mr. Shackelford says the house came into the hands of Mr. Carroll, but how he became the owner, or had a right to sell it he is unable to say." Pickens then published a letter by Dr. W. H. Wharton, written from Nashville, on March 30, 1867. In this letter, Wharton, the man who had started the church in Tuscumbia, said, "I never gave any title that I remember, for in fact I had none individually. I never opposed the Baptists or any other religious party using the house, however, at any time. We once had a church of near one hundred members. Most of them moved away or died."

Pickens continued, questioning how a transaction could take place without the knowledge of those to whom the house belonged and without any compensation for their rights. He said they made statements "that bear unmistakable evidence of fraud and falsehood." Pickens called the sale of the building a "sham sale." He then challenged Shackelford to prove the following:

- That the Baptists and other denominations ever had any rights in or title to the house in question.
- That the Christian Church ever did, either alone or in connection with others, constitute George Carroll a trustee and clothe him with the right or power to sell and convey the house.
- That Mr. Carroll did actually sell and convey to Edmund Ellet or the Baptists of Tuscumbia the house which you call the Baptist Church.
- That said Ellet or the Baptist did ever pay to those who built and owned the house the sum of $500.00 or even one dollar.
- That you Baptist of Tuscumbia can now or that you ever could produce any show of title or ownership other than your bald assertions.

The above episode shows the intense effort on the part of Pickens to regain the Tuscumbia Christian meetinghouse. Today, the Baptist church still meets on this property. The Tuscumbia Church of Christ meets in a building located beside this original property.

It was also in the year 1866 that Pickens succeeded in

reviving the church at Frankfort, Alabama. This church had ceased to meet during the Civil War. His efforts as a preacher caught the attention of gospel preacher B. F. Manire, who described Pickens as "a man of superior ability both natural and acquired." After Pickens death, Manire said, "He was unquestionably our ablest debater, and many thought our ablest preacher also."

Pickens Debate with Jacob Ditzler

Though a young man, Pickens was building a reputation as a gospel preacher, school leader, and debater. He debated Jacob Ditzler on the subject of infant baptism. The *Moulton Advertiser* issued an announcement of the debate with the following statement:

> J. A. Woodall and W. E. Cameron publishes in the Decatur paper, 'that Rev. Jacob Ditzler, of Ky., will meet Elder J. M. Pickens at McKendree church, 7 miles south east of Danville, on Thursday the 16th of October in a debate on the subject of Baptism &c.,' We should like to hear it but don't propose to ride 40 miles to enjoy so great a blessing (*Moulton Advertiser*, October 17, 1873).

Dr. Jacob Ditzler was a Methodist and the champion of the Methodist cause. He held numerous debates and probably thought the young man from Lawrence County could not be a worthy opponent in debate. If Ditzler thought this, he was badly mistaken. B. F. Manire wrote in his book, The History of the Christian Church in Mississippi, (p. 72), "The doughty Dr. (Ditzler) not expecting to find such a man in the mountains of North Alabama, had anticipated an easy victory, but was doubtless as badly disappointed as in any debate he ever held, for Pickens picked him all (to) pieces."

Excerpts of the debate were published in February 5, 1874 issue of *Southern Christian Weekly*. Ditzler, who depended greatly on history and not on scripture, met his match in the young man, Pickens.

Ditzler supported his position of infant baptism using various men from history as the authority for his position. He pointed to Tertullian, The Council of Carthage, Bishop Fidus, Origen, Father Smarius, and Orchard's Church History. Pickens said of Ditzler:

> My friend is a remarkable genius; he can prove infant baptism from the voice of history and then from its silence. Indeed, I scarcely know of any premise from which he can not draw infant baptism. He speaks of infant baptism, therefore it is authorized by the word of God. History does not speak of infant baptism, therefore it existed.

The last statement in the article was, "As was apparent to the audience, Mr. D. signally failed."

Greenback Candidate for Governor

The Greenback political party was born in the mid-1870s and was a short-lived coalition of farmers and laborers who came together to protest the federal monetary policies. This movement made allies with organized labor and managed to influence the continued printing of paper money. The Greenbacks demanded that the federal government issue an adequate supply of paper money when the supply of currency failed to keep pace with population growth. Many southerners felt this policy was detrimental to their region, which suffered from a lack of currency. The lack of currency was not so apparent in the Northeast part of the country where the nation's center of industry and finance were located.

In Alabama, the Greenback Party made bids for the state legislature, opposing the Democratic Party. In 1878, William Lowe of Huntsville, won election to the U. S.

House of Representatives as a Greenback Party candidate. In 1880, the Greenback Party ran its first candidate for governor of Alabama. James Madison Pickens of Lawrence County was selected to lead the ticket. Pickens was recognized as a leading proponent of the working class.

Pickens won the endorsement of the Republican Party in the 1880 election but still only gained 24 percent of the vote, losing the election to Rufus W. Cobb. (Cobb, elected for two terms as governor, was the president of Central Iron Works in Helena, Alabama, and was a staunch ally of mining and manufacturing interests. He also served as an attorney for the powerful Louisville and Nashville Railroad.) The reported violence, intimidation, and tampering with vote counts by the Democrats is believed to have played a large role in Pickens' poor showing. Such tactics also initially deprived Lowe of re-election to Congress, but he contested the election results and was ultimately declared the winner. Neither of these men lived much longer. The death of Pickens in 1881 remains a mystery. Some believe his death was a political assassination. Lowe died in October 1882, depriving the Alabama Greenback Party of its lone major officeholder.

The Death of J. M. Pickens

Several North Alabama newspapers carried the account of the death of J. M. Pickens. The *North Alabamian*, published in Tuscumbia, Alabama, carried a detailed article in its February 11, 1881 issue. Pickens was well known in the Tuscumbia area. He had preached in and around Tuscumbia, and one genealogical website reported that Pickens had served as president of Deshler Female Institute in Tuscumbia. Also the *North Alabamian* held similar political views as Pickens. The paper reported:

> The Rev. J. M. Pickens, late candidate for Governor of this State, and William Davidson, a

young man who lived with him, were shot last Thursday by Robt. Letson in sight of their home at Mountain Home, and Pickens killed outright and Davidson dangerously wounded.

From parties who were at the preliminary trial of Letson last Monday, we gather the following facts:

Pickens and Davison had just left the residence of Mr. French where they had gone to grind their axes. Pickens was carrying both axes and Davidson a maul. Whilst in sight of French's house they were met by Letson who stated to Pickens that Davidson had slandered his daughter and that he intended to kill him. He at once drew his pistol and shot Davidson down, the ball going through his right lung. As he attempted to shoot the second time, Pickens who had remonstrated with him, struck the pistol out of his hand with the helve of the axe. There upon a struggle for the pistol ensued and Letson regained it and commenced shooting Pickens. After the first shot, which ranged up his arm towards the elbow, he ran, pursued by Letson who fired three more shots two of which took effect in his side or back the last killing him instantly, it is supposed. He ran more than a hundred yards before he was shot the last time, Letson following him up. When the latter turned back from Pickens he was heard to say to him, 'Now get up ____ ____, if you can.' We are informed that Davidson who is still living says that on returning to him he said he would finish him, but he told him he was dying and he then passed on (sic, out). It was proved on the trial that Davidson, who will probably get well, had repeatedly circulated the most shameful and disgraceful reports about Letson's daughter.

A young man named French was the only witness to the shooting. He had gone into the house and heard the shot fired. (He saw) Pickens holding an axe up cross wise before him as if to ward off an attack, and almost at the same time he saw Letson shoot and Pickens run, and was killed as above stated.

Mr. Pickens leaves an interesting family, a wife and three children. He was a man of considerable ability and was widely known as a Campbellite Minister and a musician of a high order of talent. Little or no sympathy is expressed for Davidson, but the murder of Mr. Pickens is considered one of the most atrocious and cowardly crimes ever committed in this State. Letson was remanded to jail and was sent to this place Tuesday to await the action of the Grand Jury of Lawrence County.

Pickens' body was taken to Columbus, Mississippi, where he was buried in the Friendship Cemetery. His tombstone does not extol his virtues or honors. It simply says: James M. Pickens, born Feb. 6, 1836, died Feb. 3, 1881. When his wife, Mary, died fifteen years later, she was laid to rest beside him.

The Trial of Robert Letson

The trial of Robert Letson for the murder of J. M. Pickens was held the first week of November 1881, in Tuscumbia, Alabama. The *Moulton Advertiser* newspaper reported the following account of the trial in its November 10, 1881 edition:

> R. G. Letson was tried last week for the killing of Rev. J. M. Pickens, and found guilty of murder in the second degree and sentenced to the Penitentiary for twelve years.
> The argument of counsel on both sides were able and eloquent. Mr. J. H. Branch opened for the prosecution and in a three-quarters of an hour's speech, ably presented the strong points in the case. He was followed by Col. E. H. Foster for the defense;

who, in a masterly and eloquent speech, occupying a portion each of two days, made an earnest appeal for the life of his client. It was, perhaps, the most feeling and heart touching speech that was made during the trial. Mr. S. P. Rather then followed for the prosecution, and made a brief but forcible argument. Judge R. O. Picket closed the argument for the defense in the factious and strongly legal manner. He swept down upon the Jury and audience with power, and at times he became very eloquent, and moved every heart in sympathy toward his client. Solicitor Henry C. Jones then, in a speech that held the vast audience in profound silence for an hour, closed the argument for the State. The charge of Judge Speake was given in manuscript, with several snatches of law from the attorneys; and at one o'clock p. m. Friday the case went to the Jury and the above mentioned verdict was returned the next morning at 9 o'clock.

The widow of the deceased, with her orphan children, was present pleading for justice. The defendant's wife, slandered daughter and other children were by his side, asking for mercy.

The Jury was composed of members of all parties and churches.

From reading the above account of Letson's trial, the trial was more of persuasive speeches than law or testimony. The defense was based on a crime of passion, and for this reason Letson only received a twelve year sentence. This gave rise to outrage among Pickens' supporters and Greenback Party members. Cries of political assassination and cover-up were expressed in local newspapers. It is not known if Letson's prior criminal record was considered in the trial. According to Paul Horton's paper (mentioned later in this story), "[H]e (Letson) had been indicted for a criminal offense for which he posted bond in the fall of 1869. In 1880, the circuit court indicted him for killing or injuring an ox owned by Davidson and for 'falsely and maliciously' accusing Sarah Davidson of stealing his cotton." Horton said Letson was a violent and disturbed man. His violence and immoral behavior, especially toward his own daughter, resulted in his death when his son-in-law, shot him with a double-barreled shotgun after his release from prison.

Was Pickens Death a Political Assassination?

An excellent paper titled *The Assassination of Rev. James Madison Pickens and the Persistence of Anti-bourbon Activism in North Alabama* by Paul Horton was published by the Alabama Review, 2004. In the paper, Horton explores the evidence of political assassination as the cause of Pickens' death. Horton suggests the possibility of Letson being coaxed into killing Pickens in a "manner that would allow him to plead guilty to manslaughter or, at worst, second-degree murder," which would result in a shortened sentence. Horton suggested that Pickens murder was carried out to prevent Pickens from publishing a Greenback Party paper at this Mountain Home community. Such a paper could have been a serious blow to the Democratic Party. Horton offered evidence of oral history from the Mountain Home community that Letson's wife, after divorcing Letson, told several teachers at the Mountain Home School that Letson had told her prior to the shootings that he was going to kill Pickens and Davidson. Additional evidence that further fuels this contention is that the chairman of the Democratic Party Executive Committee for the eighth congressional district, Ephraim Hubbard Foster, served as Letson's counsel.

The assassination theory was further corroborated by the fact that there was an attempt to kill the only witness to the murder. John French, who witnessed the murder, was shot at while standing at the back door of his house. The shot, fired from the nearby woods, resulted in a bullet in the weather boarding of the French house. An examination of the bullet showed that the bullet had been hollowed out and filled with axle grease. Those who know anything about firearms and ammunition know that hollowed out bullets are meant to spread out on contact and promote the greatest amount of damage. Letson was in jail at the time. This gives additional evidence that Letson did not act alone. Paul Horton's paper states, "A story originally printed in the *Hartselle Sentinel* and reprinted in the *Huntsville Advocate* maintained that the murder was premeditated and amounted to a political assassination."

In 1945, gospel preacher Asa Plyler traveled the state of Alabama, studying and recording history of the churches of Christ. (His writings have recently been published in a book, Historical Sketches of the churches of Christ in Alabama.) In the summer of 1945, he came to Mountain Home to inquire if anyone could remember anything about the school at Mountain Home, or about James Madison Pickens. He stopped at a store and inquired if anyone in the community knew anything about the school or Pickens. He was told of an elderly lady who might help him. The woman, eighty-two years old, had lived at Mountain Home all her life. When asked about Pickens, the old lady's face lighted up with a smile. She replied, "I most certainly do, and do I remember him, he was my teacher." The woman continued to tell of the death of Pickens, which differed from the newspaper account. Plyler perhaps was surprised to find out that this woman was the sister of William Davidson, the man shot at the same time as Pickens. She said that her brother was the printer for Pickens and that Pickens was enlarging his printing office at the time of his death. She said he had just bought a new and larger printing press for publishing a paper. She stated that the man who killed Pickens came up to the shop and said:

> I am not going to have any paper published here. He pulled a pistol from his pocket and shot my brother one time. When he fell, brother Pickens

began to beg him not to shoot him any more. The man then shot brother Pickens in the arm and as he turned away he then shot him four times in the back, he fell in the road and was dead within a few minutes. No cause was ever given except that no paper was going to be published there.

This account is in agreement with the statement in Paul Horton's paper that Letson was heard to say that he "would ride fifty miles to kill a man who would publish such political matter as that contained in a copy of the *Huntsville Advocate*, which a man had been reading to him." It may have been widely known that Pickens was going to publish a paper, and that the paper would put the Democratic Party in a bad light while promoting the Greenback Party.

Did members of the Democratic Party have Pickens killed? "Dirty" and "politics" are two words that have long been associated in describing Alabama politics. This writer has a friend who was beaten with an axe handle while serving as a poll watcher for the Republican Party as late as 1966.

Conspiracy or conspiracy theory? There is evidence for a cover-up of a political assassination.

Death of Robert Letson

On Robert Letson's release from prison, he sexually assaulted his own daughter, Elizabeth Letson Goodwin, shortly after she married Thomas Goodwin. He then threatened to kill his son-in-law, Thomas Goodwin. *The Courtland Enterprise* newspaper reported the following:

> Friday, November 11, 1898—R. G. Letson, of Mountain Home, was shot and instantly killed by his son-in-law, Thomas Goodwin, on last Thursday evening, at the home of Harvey Wright, about four miles from here. It seems that some family trouble had arisen between the two, and Goodwin left

Letson's house about a month ago. On Thursday Letson went to look for Goodwin—for what cause is not known—but Goodwin fearing trouble was prepared for him and on sight shot him with a double barrel shotgun, loaded with buck shot, seventeen of which took effect killing Letson instantly. The facts in the case, no doubt will all come out at the preliminary trial, which is set for Monday next.

It only took one week for a preliminary trial to determine that Thomas Goodwin had acted in self-defense. *The Courtland Enterprise*, Friday, November 18, 1898 reported:

> In the preliminary trial, on Monday last, of Tommie Goodwin, charged with murder in the first degree, in the killing of R. G. Letson, before Squires W. R. Aycock and Jno. A. Gilchrist, was acquitted. The defense was represented by Hon. C. M. Sherrod, and he made out a clear case of self-defense, not only so, but the State witnesses made it a clear case of justifiable homicide.

Epilogue

The death of James Madison Pickens left Mrs. Pickens and her children without means of support. Gospel preacher B. F. Manire wrote from Saltillo, Mississippi on August 31, 1882, a plea published in *The Christian Standard*, September 1882, that a fund was being established for the Pickens' family. He wrote:

> The death of Bro. Pickens was a calamity to the cause at large, and especially to the cause in these two States. He was unquestionably our ablest debater, and many thought our ablest preacher also. He lost his own life in saving the life of another man, a young man in his employment. I knew him from his boyhood, and have known his wife from her

childhood. Her father and mother were for many years strong pillers (sic) in the church at Columbus, Miss.

Sister Pickens is in feeble health, in destitute circumstances, and has four small children to be raised and educated. She has four sisters and one brother, all of whom, with their companions, would, I am sure, share most freely their last crust of bread with her and her helpless children; but their means are limited, and they have children of their own to raise and educate, and can not do all that needs to be done. The church at Columbus, I feel assured, will manifest a commendable liberality, but the church itself is weak both financially and numerically, and needs help to do the church work that ought to be done in Columbus. Sister Pickens needs help not only to carry her through the coming winter, but through several coming years, until her boys are large enough and well enough educated to make a living for her and themselves.

Manire pointed out in this article that Mrs. Pickens had "an agency" to sell the book, "<u>Home Life of Alexander Campbell</u>," a book written by Mrs. Alexander Campbell. Christians were urged to purchase this book, from which Mrs. Pickens would receive a commission. He also submitted a copy of a newspaper article from the Courtland, Alabama *Sentinel*, which carried the announcement of the Pickens' Children Fund. In part, the article stated:

The object of the Pickens Orphan Fund, as has been previously stated is to raise a sum of money sufficient to educate Mr. Pickens' four fatherless children. It is needless to say had he lived no appeal like this would have been made; but since he was brutally murdered by an individual whom he never wronged, we think it obligatory upon the members of the Christian church, of which he was an able and honored minister, to see that his children are properly educated,. It can be done by contributions to the

Pickens Orphan Fund, the officers of which are high-toned gentlemen, who will see that every cent given is used for the object indicated.

All monies received will be deposited in a saving bank, and the interest thereon used for the purpose of educating these four bright and promising children.

Every member of the Christian Church should contribute his or her mite, and ere long we will all be rejoiced at the great good that will have been accomplished.

Mary Pickens would live another fifteen years before her death in 1896. J. M. and Mary had six children. Two preceded J. M. in death. James Madison Pickens, Jr., born in 1872, left home at age 13 and held a civil service position in Washington, D. C. for many years. He died in 1963 in Chevy Chase, Maryland. Sallie Pickens married and lived in Birmingham, Alabama. No date of death is known. William Pickens died in 1936 in Los Angeles, California. Carrie Pickens also married and settled in Birmingham, Alabama. The date of her death is not known.

William Davidson, who was shot by Robert Letson at the time Pickens was killed, survived the attack. According to Paul Horton, Davidson, later became a renowned surgeon with substantial property in Montana and California."

Final Word

The American Restoration Movement of the Nineteenth Century is a story of trials and struggles of those committed to restoring New Testament Christianity. They believed that the Holy Bible was the inerrant, all-sufficient, God-breathed revelation of God to man. They accepted the Bible alone (without Creed or Discipline) as the only foundation on which the New Testament church could be restored.

This collection of short stories is dedicated to the memory of these self-sacrificing men and women who gave their lives for a cause they deemed greater than life itself. Often the stories center around the men of the restoration movement and their sacrifice of the comforts of home and family to go forth, many times for weeks or months at a time, preaching and teaching the word of God. But let us never forget the wives of these men who worked harder than many men, cooking, farming, rearing children, suffering, and dying for the cause of Christ. When their husbands were away for extended periods, these godly women were both mother and father to the children. Many of them died at a relatively young age. Never forget the sacrifice of these women for the cause of Christ and His church.

The passing of each year provides additional challenges for those researching the history of churches and the men and women of the restoration movement. We are a year further away from the history that we are exploring, and every year information is thrown away because it is considered useless by someone who has no interest in the past. Our desire is to preserve information about those who have come before us. We urge church members to write the histories of the churches where they attend in order to preserve the past and the present for those in the future.

www.ingramcontent.com/pod-product-compliance
Lightning Source LLC
LaVergne TN
LVHW021702060526
838200LV00050B/2472